THIS BOOK BELONGS TO:

CONTACT INFORMATION	
NAME:	
ADDRESS:	
PHONE:	

START / END DATES

_____ / _____ / _____ TO _____ / _____ / _____

DEDICATION

This book is dedicated to all the energetic Goat Owners out there who want to keep record of their goats information.

You are my inspiration for producing books and I'm honored to be a part of keeping all of your Goat notes and records organized.

This journal notebook will help you record your details about your goats' pedigree, breeding and kidding.

Thoughtfully put together with these sections to record: Goat Information, Medical Information, Doe's Kidding Record, Buck's Record

Of Progeny, Goat Record and Milk Production.

HOW TO USE THIS BOOK:

The purpose of this book is to keep all of your Goat notes all in one place. It will help keep you organized.

This Goat Log will allow you to accurately document every detail about your goats and also track medical and kidding. It's a great way to chart your course as you care for your goats.

Here are examples of the prompts for you to fill in and write about your experience in this book:

Goat Information:

Place To Attach Photo
Name, Breed, Birth Date, Buck Or Doe
Date Acquired, From Where
Purpose, Colors, Identifying Marks
Blank Lined Notes
Pedigree Chart
Medical Information:

Injury Or Illness
Parasite Control
Testing Record
Vaccination & Supplement Record
Doe's Kidding Record:

Doe's Name, Date Breed, Kidding Date
Number Of Kids, Sex D/B, Name Of Kid
Sire Of Kid
Weight, Tattoo
Buck's Record Of Progeny:

Buck's Name
Year, Breed To
Kids, D/B
Goat Record:

Goat's Name, Breed, Date Of Birth
Date Weaned, Identification
Weight By Month
Feed Record By Month (Grain, Field or Pasture)
Milk Production:

By Month
Yearly Total Milk Produced

GOAT INFORMATION

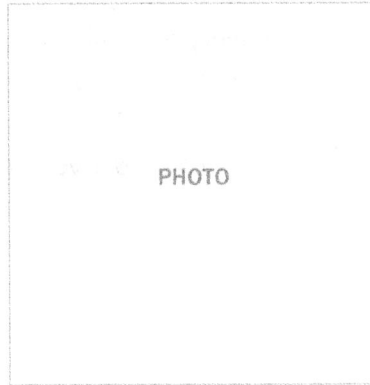

PHOTO

NAME		☐ BUCK	☐ DOE
BREED		BIRTH DATE:	
DATE ACQUIRED:	HOW ACQUIRED: ☐ BORN ON FARM ☐ PURCHASED ☐ LEASED		
COLORS / IDENTIFYING MARKS:			
PURPOSE: ☐ MILK ☐ MEAT ☐ PET ☐ OTHER			

PEDIGREE CHART

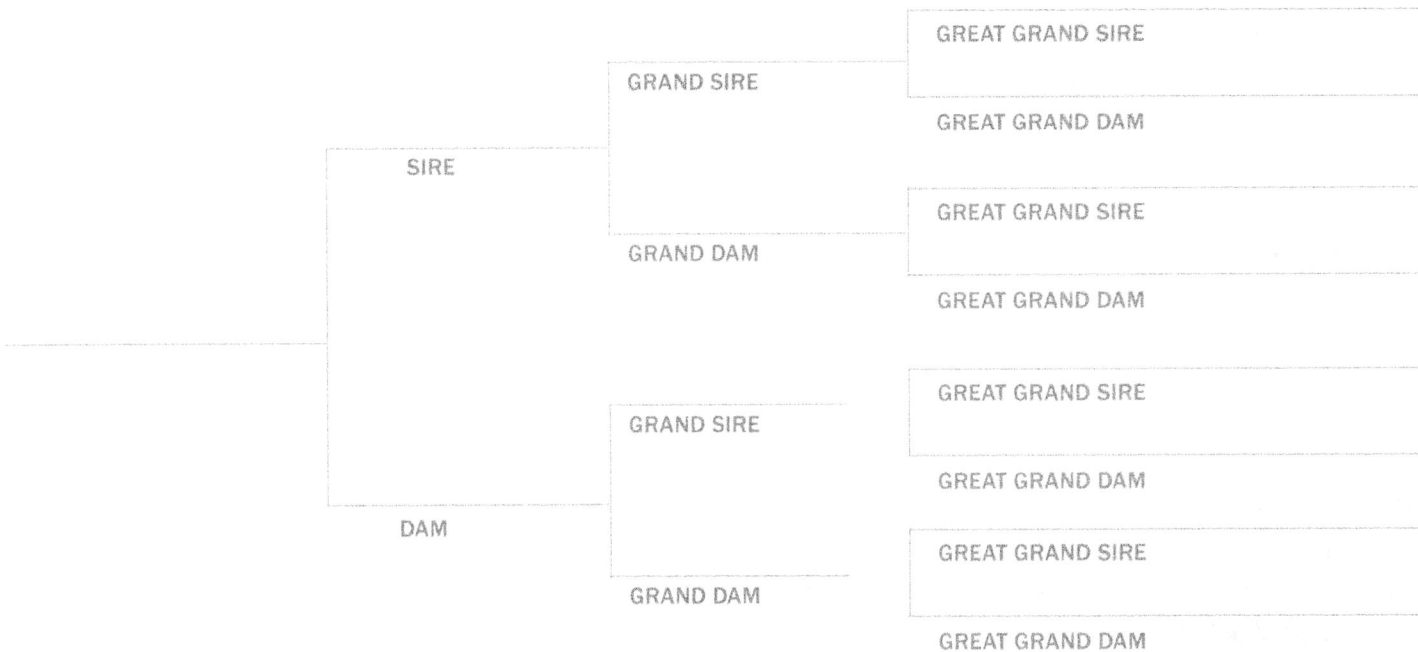

```
                                                          GREAT GRAND SIRE
                                      GRAND SIRE
                                                          GREAT GRAND DAM
                   SIRE
                                                          GREAT GRAND SIRE
                                      GRAND DAM
                                                          GREAT GRAND DAM

                                                          GREAT GRAND SIRE
                                      GRAND SIRE
                                                          GREAT GRAND DAM
                   DAM
                                                          GREAT GRAND SIRE
                                      GRAND DAM
                                                          GREAT GRAND DAM
```

MEDICAL INFORMATION

INJURY OR ILLNESS

DATE	DESCRIPTION OR NATURE OF ILLNESS	TREATMENT

PARASITE CONTROL

DATE	METHOD OR DEWORMER	DATE	METHOD OR DEWORMER

TESTING RECORD

DATE	TEST PERFORMED (CAE, CL, TB...)	RESULT	DATE	TEST PERFORMED (CAE, CL, TB...)	RESULT

VACCINATION & SUPPLEMENT RECORD

DATE	TARGET DISEASE	DRUG OR SUPPLEMENT USED	DOSAGE	RESULTS

DOE'S KIDDING RECORD

DOE'S NAME:	

DATE BREED	KIDDING DATE	# OF KIDS	SEX D/B	NAME OF KID	SIRE OF KID	WEIGHT	TATTOO

BUCK'S RECORD OF PROGENY

DOE'S NAME:

YEAR	BRED TO	KIDS	DOE/BUCK

GOAT RECORD

GOAT'S NAME:		IDENTIFICATION:	
BREED:	DATE OF BIRTH:		DATE OF WEANED:

WEIGHT (POUNDS)

BIRTH	JAN	FEB	MAR	APR	MAY	JUN	JUL	AUG	SEP	OCT	NOV	DEC	FINAL

FEED RECORD

	JAN	FEB	MAR	APR	MAY	JUN	JUL	AUG	SEP	OCT	NOV	DEC	TOTAL
GRAIN													
GRAIN													
PASTURE													

MILK PRODUCTION

DOE'S NAME:		IDENTIFICATION:	
BREED:	DATE OF BIRTH:	KIDDING DATE:	

JANUARY		AVERAGE LBS / DAY X 31 DAYS =		LBS
FEBRUARY		AVERAGE LBS / DAY X 31 DAYS =		LBS
MARCH		AVERAGE LBS / DAY X 31 DAYS =		LBS
APRIL		AVERAGE LBS / DAY X 31 DAYS =		LBS
MAY		AVERAGE LBS / DAY X 31 DAYS =		LBS
JUNE		AVERAGE LBS / DAY X 31 DAYS =		LBS
JULY		AVERAGE LBS / DAY X 31 DAYS =		LBS
AUGUST		AVERAGE LBS / DAY X 31 DAYS =		LBS
SEPTEMBER		AVERAGE LBS / DAY X 31 DAYS =		LBS
OCTOBER		AVERAGE LBS / DAY X 31 DAYS =		LBS
NOVEMBER		AVERAGE LBS / DAY X 31 DAYS =		LBS
DECEMBER		AVERAGE LBS / DAY X 31 DAYS =		LBS
YEARLY TOTAL MILK PRODUCED =				LBS

TOTAL VALUE OF MILK PRODUCED FOR THE YEAR

	LBS X $		VALUE PER LBS =	

GOAT INFORMATION

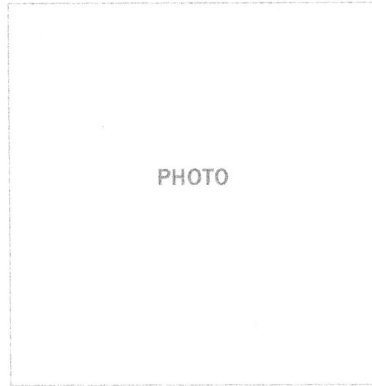

PHOTO

NAME	☐ BUCK	☐ DOE
BREED	BIRTH DATE:	

DATE ACQUIRED: | HOW ACQUIRED: ☐ BORN ON FARM ☐ PURCHASED ☐ LEASED

COLORS / IDENTIFYING MARKS:

PURPOSE: ☐ MILK ☐ MEAT ☐ PET ☐ OTHER

PEDIGREE CHART

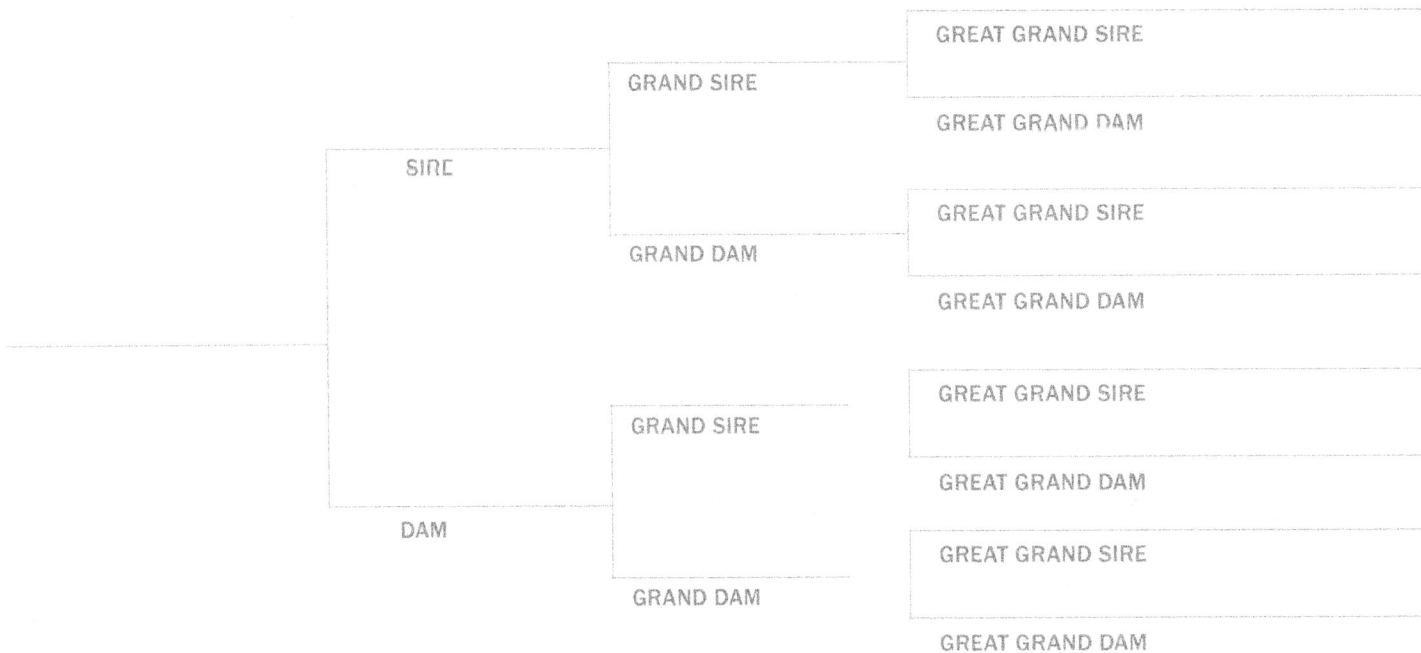

SIRE

GRAND SIRE

GREAT GRAND SIRE

GREAT GRAND DAM

GRAND DAM

GREAT GRAND SIRE

GREAT GRAND DAM

DAM

GRAND SIRE

GREAT GRAND SIRE

GREAT GRAND DAM

GRAND DAM

GREAT GRAND SIRE

GREAT GRAND DAM

MEDICAL INFORMATION

INJURY OR ILLNESS

DATE	DESCRIPTION OR NATURE OF ILLNESS	TREATMENT

PARASITE CONTROL

DATE	METHOD OR DEWORMER	DATE	METHOD OR DEWORMER

TESTING RECORD

DATE	TEST PERFORMED (CAE, CL, TB...)	RESULT	DATE	TEST PERFORMED (CAE, CL, TB...)	RESULT

VACCINATION & SUPPLEMENT RECORD

DATE	TARGET DISEASE	DRUG OR SUPPLEMENT USED	DOSAGE	RESULTS

DOE'S KIDDING RECORD

DOE'S NAME:

DATE BREED	KIDDING DATE	# OF KIDS	SEX D/B	NAME OF KID	SIRE OF KID	WEIGHT	TATTOO

BUCK'S RECORD OF PROGENY

DOE'S NAME:

YEAR	BRED TO	KIDS	DOE/BUCK

GOAT RECORD

GOAT'S NAME:

IDENTIFICATION:

BREED:

DATE OF BIRTH:

DATE OF WEANED:

WEIGHT (POUNDS)

BIRTH	JAN	FEB	MAR	APR	MAY	JUN	JUL	AUG	SEP	OCT	NOV	DEC	FINAL

FEED RECORD

	JAN	FEB	MAR	APR	MAY	JUN	JUL	AUG	SEP	OCT	NOV	DEC	TOTAL
GRAIN													
GRAIN													
PASTURE													

MILK PRODUCTION

DOE'S NAME: | IDENTIFICATION:

BREED: | DATE OF BIRTH: | KIDDING DATE:

JANUARY		AVERAGE LBS / DAY X 31 DAYS =		LBS
FEBRUARY		AVERAGE LBS / DAY X 31 DAYS =		LBS
MARCH		AVERAGE LBS / DAY X 31 DAYS =		LBS
APRIL		AVERAGE LBS / DAY X 31 DAYS =		LBS
MAY		AVERAGE LBS / DAY X 31 DAYS =		LBS
JUNE		AVERAGE LBS / DAY X 31 DAYS =		LBS
JULY		AVERAGE LBS / DAY X 31 DAYS =		LBS
AUGUST		AVERAGE LBS / DAY X 31 DAYS =		LBS
SEPTEMBER		AVERAGE LBS / DAY X 31 DAYS =		LBS
OCTOBER		AVERAGE LBS / DAY X 31 DAYS =		LBS
NOVEMBER		AVERAGE LBS / DAY X 31 DAYS =		LBS
DECEMBER		AVERAGE LBS / DAY X 31 DAYS =		LBS
YEARLY TOTAL MILK PRODUCED =				LBS

TOTAL VALUE OF MILK PRODUCED FOR THE YEAR

LBS X $		VALUE PER LBS =	

GOAT INFORMATION

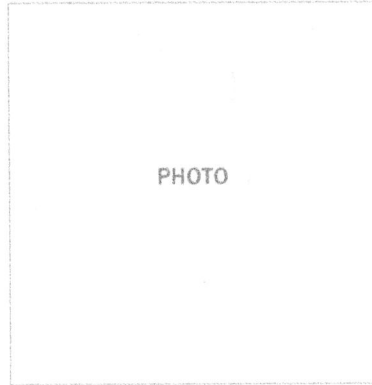

PHOTO

NAME	☐ BUCK	☐ DOE
BREED	BIRTH DATE:	
DATE ACQUIRED:	HOW ACQUIRED: ☐ BORN ON FARM ☐ PURCHASED ☐ LEASED	
COLORS / IDENTIFYING MARKS:		

PURPOSE: ☐ MILK ☐ MEAT ☐ PET ☐ OTHER

PEDIGREE CHART

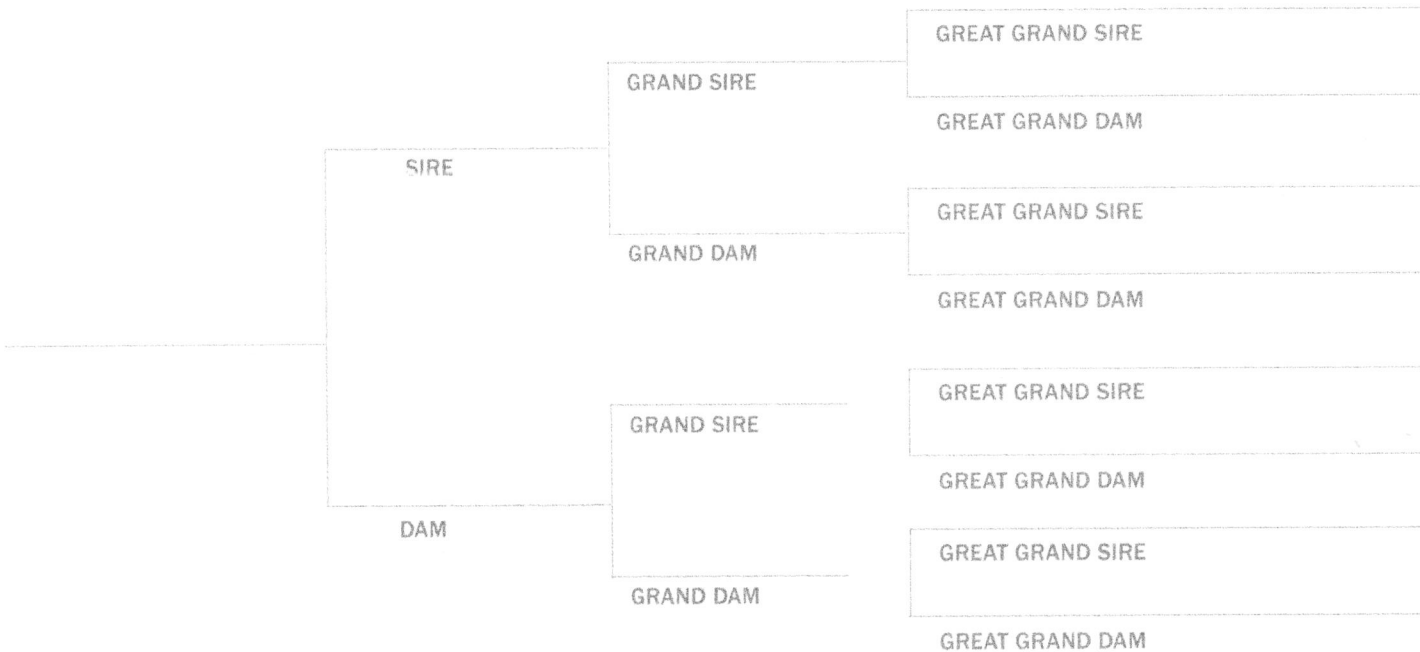

			GREAT GRAND SIRE
		GRAND SIRE	GREAT GRAND DAM
	SIRE		GREAT GRAND SIRE
		GRAND DAM	GREAT GRAND DAM
			GREAT GRAND SIRE
		GRAND SIRE	GREAT GRAND DAM
	DAM		GREAT GRAND SIRE
		GRAND DAM	GREAT GRAND DAM

MEDICAL INFORMATION

INJURY OR ILLNESS

DATE	DESCRIPTION OR NATURE OF ILLNESS	TREATMENT

PARASITE CONTROL

DATE	METHOD OR DEWORMER	DATE	METHOD OR DEWORMER

TESTING RECORD

DATE	TEST PERFORMED (CAE, CL, TB...)	RESULT	DATE	TEST PERFORMED (CAE, CL, TB...)	RESULT

VACCINATION & SUPPLEMENT RECORD

DATE	TARGET DISEASE	DRUG OR SUPPLEMENT USED	DOSAGE	RESULTS

DOE'S KIDDING RECORD

DOE'S NAME:

DATE BREED	KIDDING DATE	# OF KIDS	SEX D/B	NAME OF KID	SIRE OF KID	WEIGHT	TATTOO

BUCK'S RECORD OF PROGENY

DOE'S NAME:

YEAR	BRED TO	KIDS	DOE/BUCK

GOAT RECORD

GOAT'S NAME:		IDENTIFICATION:	
BREED:	DATE OF BIRTH:		DATE OF WEANED:

WEIGHT (POUNDS)

BIRTH	JAN	FEB	MAR	APR	MAY	JUN	JUL	AUG	SEP	OCT	NOV	DEC	FINAL

FEED RECORD

	JAN	FEB	MAR	APR	MAY	JUN	JUL	AUG	SEP	OCT	NOV	DEC	TOTAL
GRAIN													
GRAIN													
PASTURE													

MILK PRODUCTION

DOE'S NAME:		IDENTIFICATION:	
BREED:	DATE OF BIRTH:	KIDDING DATE:	

JANUARY		AVERAGE LBS / DAY X 31 DAYS =		LBS
FEBRUARY		AVERAGE LBS / DAY X 31 DAYS =		LBS
MARCH		AVERAGE LBS / DAY X 31 DAYS =		LBS
APRIL		AVERAGE LBS / DAY X 31 DAYS =		LBS
MAY		AVERAGE LBS / DAY X 31 DAYS =		LBS
JUNE		AVERAGE LBS / DAY X 31 DAYS =		LBS
JULY		AVERAGE LBS / DAY X 31 DAYS =		LBS
AUGUST		AVERAGE LBS / DAY X 31 DAYS =		LBS
SEPTEMBER		AVERAGE LBS / DAY X 31 DAYS =		LBS
OCTOBER		AVERAGE LBS / DAY X 31 DAYS =		LBS
NOVEMBER		AVERAGE LBS / DAY X 31 DAYS =		LBS
DECEMBER		AVERAGE LBS / DAY X 31 DAYS =		LBS
YEARLY TOTAL MILK PRODUCED =				LBS

TOTAL VALUE OF MILK PRODUCED FOR THE YEAR

	LBS X $		VALUE PER LBS =	

GOAT INFORMATION

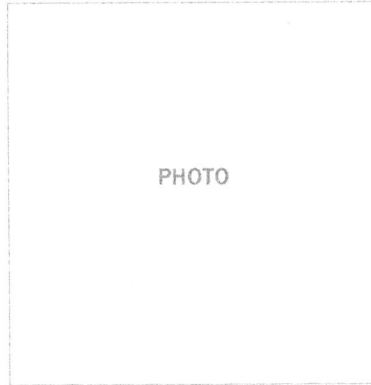

PHOTO

NAME	☐ BUCK	☐ DOE
BREED	BIRTH DATE:	
DATE ACQUIRED:	HOW ACQUIRED: ☐ BORN ON FARM ☐ PURCHASED ☐ LEASED	
COLORS / IDENTIFYING MARKS:		
PURPOSE: ☐ MILK ☐ MEAT ☐ PET ☐ OTHER		

PEDIGREE CHART

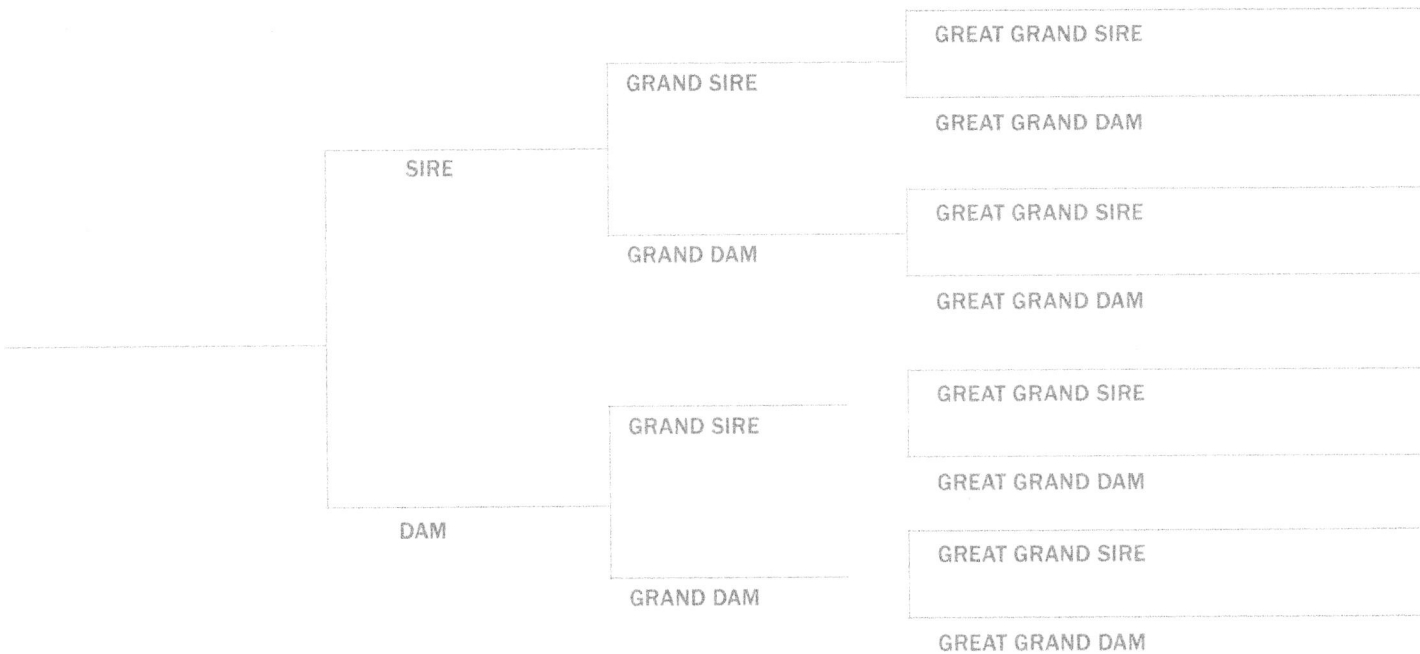

SIRE

- GRAND SIRE
  - GREAT GRAND SIRE
  - GREAT GRAND DAM
- GRAND DAM
  - GREAT GRAND SIRE
  - GREAT GRAND DAM

DAM

- GRAND SIRE
  - GREAT GRAND SIRE
  - GREAT GRAND DAM
- GRAND DAM
  - GREAT GRAND SIRE
  - GREAT GRAND DAM

MEDICAL INFORMATION

INJURY OR ILLNESS

DATE	DESCRIPTION OR NATURE OF ILLNESS	TREATMENT

PARASITE CONTROL

DATE	METHOD OR DEWORMER	DATE	METHOD OR DEWORMER

TESTING RECORD

DATE	TEST PERFORMED (CAE, CL, TB...)	RESULT	DATE	TEST PERFORMED (CAE, CL, TB...)	RESULT

VACCINATION & SUPPLEMENT RECORD

DATE	TARGET DISEASE	DRUG OR SUPPLEMENT USED	DOSAGE	RESULTS

DOE'S KIDDING RECORD

DOE'S NAME:

DATE BREED	KIDDING DATE	# OF KIDS	SEX D/B	NAME OF KID	SIRE OF KID	WEIGHT	TATTOO

BUCK'S RECORD OF PROGENY

DOE'S NAME:

YEAR	BRED TO	KIDS	DOE/BUCK

GOAT RECORD

GOAT'S NAME:		IDENTIFICATION:	
BREED:	DATE OF BIRTH:	DATE OF WEANED:	

WEIGHT (POUNDS)

BIRTH	JAN	FEB	MAR	APR	MAY	JUN	JUL	AUG	SEP	OCT	NOV	DEC	FINAL

FEED RECORD

	JAN	FEB	MAR	APR	MAY	JUN	JUL	AUG	SEP	OCT	NOV	DEC	TOTAL
GRAIN													
GRAIN													
PASTURE													

MILK PRODUCTION

DOE'S NAME:		IDENTIFICATION:	
BREED:	DATE OF BIRTH:	KIDDING DATE:	

JANUARY		AVERAGE LBS / DAY X 31 DAYS =		LBS
FEBRUARY		AVERAGE LBS / DAY X 31 DAYS =		LBS
MARCH		AVERAGE LBS / DAY X 31 DAYS =		LBS
APRIL		AVERAGE LBS / DAY X 31 DAYS =		LBS
MAY		AVERAGE LBS / DAY X 31 DAYS =		LBS
JUNE		AVERAGE LBS / DAY X 31 DAYS =		LBS
JULY		AVERAGE LBS / DAY X 31 DAYS =		LBS
AUGUST		AVERAGE LBS / DAY X 31 DAYS =		LBS
SEPTEMBER		AVERAGE LBS / DAY X 31 DAYS =		LBS
OCTOBER		AVERAGE LBS / DAY X 31 DAYS =		LBS
NOVEMBER		AVERAGE LBS / DAY X 31 DAYS =		LBS
DECEMBER		AVERAGE LBS / DAY X 31 DAYS =		LBS
YEARLY TOTAL MILK PRODUCED =				LBS

TOTAL VALUE OF MILK PRODUCED FOR THE YEAR

	LBS X $		VALUE PER LBS =	

GOAT INFORMATION

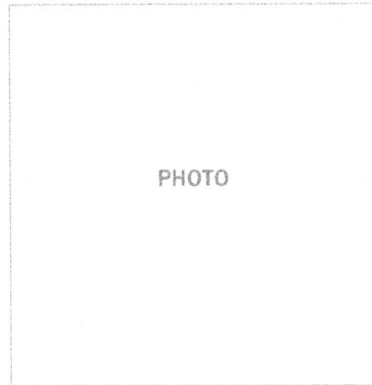

PHOTO

NAME	☐ BUCK	☐ DOE
BREED	BIRTH DATE:	

DATE ACQUIRED:	HOW ACQUIRED: ☐ BORN ON FARM ☐ PURCHASED ☐ LEASED

COLORS / IDENTIFYING MARKS:

PURPOSE:	☐ MILK	☐ MEAT	☐ PET	☐ OTHER

PEDIGREE CHART

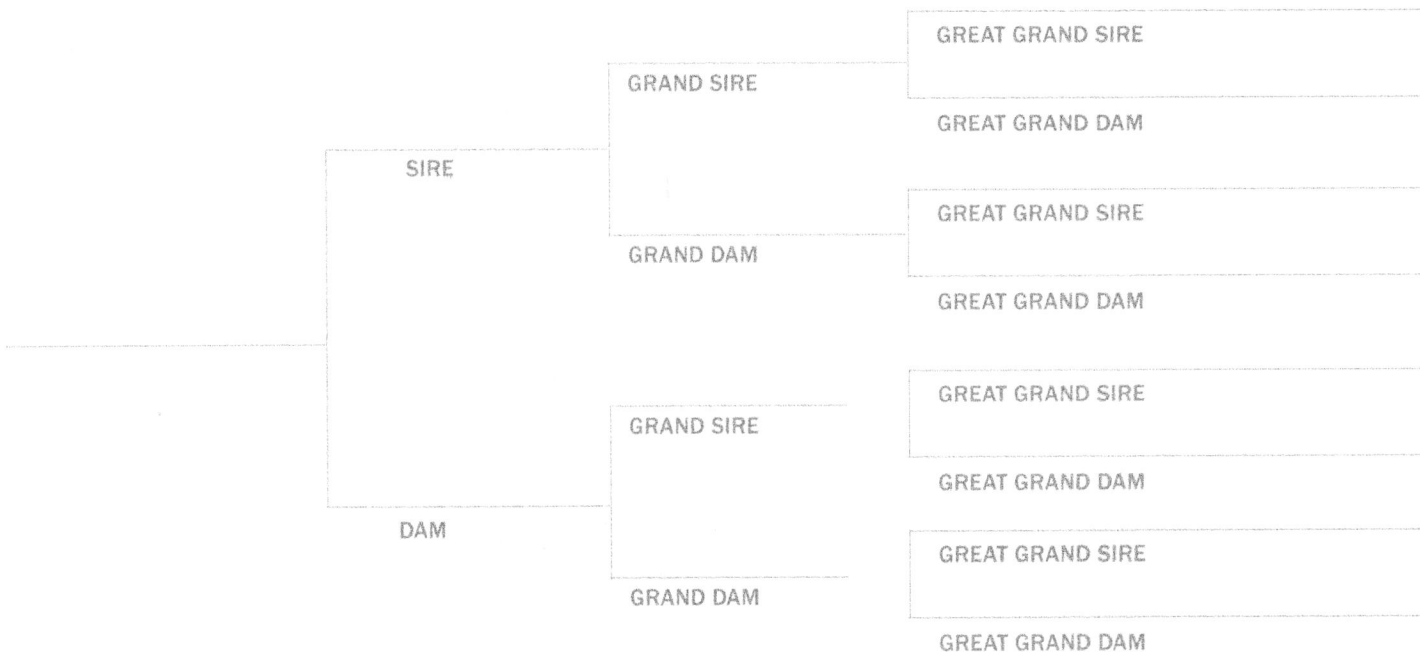

- SIRE
  - GRAND SIRE
    - GREAT GRAND SIRE
    - GREAT GRAND DAM
  - GRAND DAM
    - GREAT GRAND SIRE
    - GREAT GRAND DAM
- DAM
  - GRAND SIRE
    - GREAT GRAND SIRE
    - GREAT GRAND DAM
  - GRAND DAM
    - GREAT GRAND SIRE
    - GREAT GRAND DAM

MEDICAL INFORMATION

INJURY OR ILLNESS

DATE	DESCRIPTION OR NATURE OF ILLNESS	TREATMENT

PARASITE CONTROL

DATE	METHOD OR DEWORMER	DATE	METHOD OR DEWORMER

TESTING RECORD

DATE	TEST PERFORMED (CAE, CL, TB...)	RESULT	DATE	TEST PERFORMED (CAE, CL, TB...)	RESULT

VACCINATION & SUPPLEMENT RECORD

DATE	TARGET DISEASE	DRUG OR SUPPLEMENT USED	DOSAGE	RESULTS

DOE'S KIDDING RECORD

DOE'S NAME:

DATE BREED	KIDDING DATE	# OF KIDS	SEX D/B	NAME OF KID	SIRE OF KID	WEIGHT	TATTOO

BUCK'S RECORD OF PROGENY

DOE'S NAME:

YEAR	BRED TO	KIDS	DOE/BUCK

GOAT RECORD

GOAT'S NAME:		IDENTIFICATION:	
BREED:	DATE OF BIRTH:		DATE OF WEANED:

WEIGHT (POUNDS)

BIRTH	JAN	FEB	MAR	APR	MAY	JUN	JUL	AUG	SEP	OCT	NOV	DEC	FINAL

FEED RECORD

	JAN	FEB	MAR	APR	MAY	JUN	JUL	AUG	SEP	OCT	NOV	DEC	TOTAL
GRAIN													
GRAIN													
PASTURE													

MILK PRODUCTION

DOE'S NAME:		IDENTIFICATION:	
BREED:	DATE OF BIRTH:	KIDDING DATE:	

JANUARY		AVERAGE LBS / DAY X 31 DAYS =		LBS
FEBRUARY		AVERAGE LBS / DAY X 31 DAYS =		LBS
MARCH		AVERAGE LBS / DAY X 31 DAYS =		LBS
APRIL		AVERAGE LBS / DAY X 31 DAYS =		LBS
MAY		AVERAGE LBS / DAY X 31 DAYS =		LBS
JUNE		AVERAGE LBS / DAY X 31 DAYS =		LBS
JULY		AVERAGE LBS / DAY X 31 DAYS =		LBS
AUGUST		AVERAGE LBS / DAY X 31 DAYS =		LBS
SEPTEMBER		AVERAGE LBS / DAY X 31 DAYS =		LBS
OCTOBER		AVERAGE LBS / DAY X 31 DAYS =		LBS
NOVEMBER		AVERAGE LBS / DAY X 31 DAYS =		LBS
DECEMBER		AVERAGE LBS / DAY X 31 DAYS =		LBS
YEARLY TOTAL MILK PRODUCED =				LBS

TOTAL VALUE OF MILK PRODUCED FOR THE YEAR

LBS X $		VALUE PER LBS =	

GOAT INFORMATION

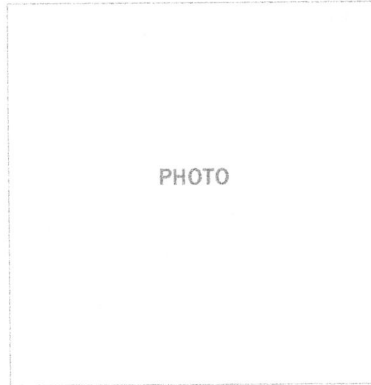

PHOTO

NAME		☐ BUCK	☐ DOE
BREED		BIRTH DATE:	
DATE ACQUIRED:	HOW ACQUIRED: ☐ BORN ON FARM ☐ PURCHASED ☐ LEASED		
COLORS / IDENTIFYING MARKS:			
PURPOSE: ☐ MILK ☐ MEAT ☐ PET ☐ OTHER			

PEDIGREE CHART

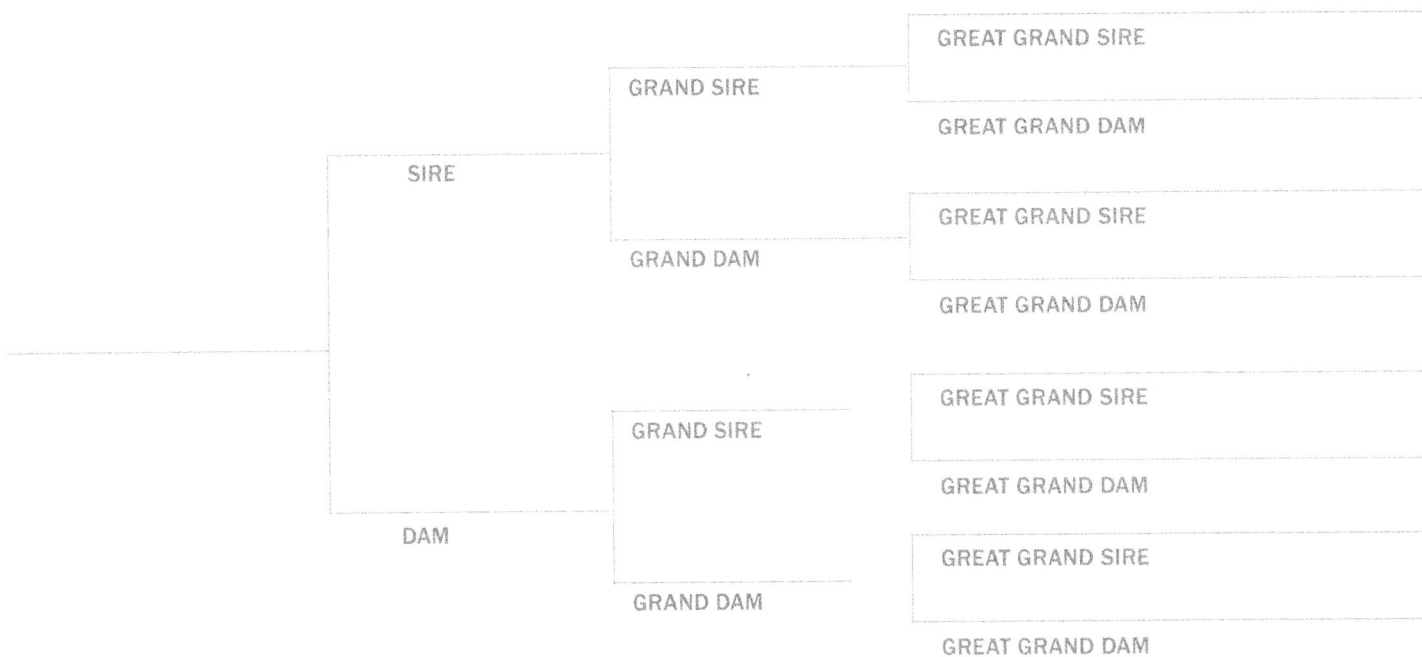

			GREAT GRAND SIRE
		GRAND SIRE	GREAT GRAND DAM
	SIRE		GREAT GRAND SIRE
		GRAND DAM	GREAT GRAND DAM
			GREAT GRAND SIRE
		GRAND SIRE	GREAT GRAND DAM
	DAM		GREAT GRAND SIRE
		GRAND DAM	GREAT GRAND DAM

MEDICAL INFORMATION

INJURY OR ILLNESS

DATE	DESCRIPTION OR NATURE OF ILLNESS	TREATMENT

PARASITE CONTROL

DATE	METHOD OR DEWORMER	DATE	METHOD OR DEWORMER

TESTING RECORD

DATE	TEST PERFORMED (CAE, CL, TB...)	RESULT	DATE	TEST PERFORMED (CAE, CL, TB...)	RESULT

VACCINATION & SUPPLEMENT RECORD

DATE	TARGET DISEASE	DRUG OR SUPPLEMENT USED	DOSAGE	RESULTS

DOE'S KIDDING RECORD

DOE'S NAME:

DATE BREED	KIDDING DATE	# OF KIDS	SEX D/B	NAME OF KID	SIRE OF KID	WEIGHT	TATTOO

BUCK'S RECORD OF PROGENY

DOE'S NAME:

YEAR	BRED TO	KIDS	DOE/BUCK

GOAT RECORD

GOAT'S NAME:		IDENTIFICATION:	
BREED:	DATE OF BIRTH:		DATE OF WEANED:

WEIGHT (POUNDS)

BIRTH	JAN	FEB	MAR	APR	MAY	JUN	JUL	AUG	SEP	OCT	NOV	DEC	FINAL

FEED RECORD

	JAN	FEB	MAR	APR	MAY	JUN	JUL	AUG	SEP	OCT	NOV	DEC	TOTAL
GRAIN													
GRAIN													
PASTURE													

MILK PRODUCTION

DOE'S NAME:		IDENTIFICATION:	
BREED:	DATE OF BIRTH:	KIDDING DATE:	

JANUARY		AVERAGE LBS / DAY X 31 DAYS =		LBS
FEBRUARY		AVERAGE LBS / DAY X 31 DAYS =		LBS
MARCH		AVERAGE LBS / DAY X 31 DAYS =		LBS
APRIL		AVERAGE LBS / DAY X 31 DAYS =		LBS
MAY		AVERAGE LBS / DAY X 31 DAYS =		LBS
JUNE		AVERAGE LBS / DAY X 31 DAYS =		LBS
JULY		AVERAGE LBS / DAY X 31 DAYS =		LBS
AUGUST		AVERAGE LBS / DAY X 31 DAYS =		LBS
SEPTEMBER		AVERAGE LBS / DAY X 31 DAYS =		LBS
OCTOBER		AVERAGE LBS / DAY X 31 DAYS =		LBS
NOVEMBER		AVERAGE LBS / DAY X 31 DAYS =		LBS
DECEMBER		AVERAGE LBS / DAY X 31 DAYS =		LBS
YEARLY TOTAL MILK PRODUCED =				LBS

TOTAL VALUE OF MILK PRODUCED FOR THE YEAR

	LBS X $		VALUE PER LBS =

GOAT INFORMATION

PHOTO

NAME	☐ BUCK	☐ DOE
BREED	BIRTH DATE:	

DATE ACQUIRED: | HOW ACQUIRED: ☐ BORN ON FARM ☐ PURCHASED ☐ LEASED

COLORS / IDENTIFYING MARKS:

PURPOSE: ☐ MILK ☐ MEAT ☐ PET ☐ OTHER

PEDIGREE CHART

- SIRE
  - GRAND SIRE
    - GREAT GRAND SIRE
    - GREAT GRAND DAM
  - GRAND DAM
    - GREAT GRAND SIRE
    - GREAT GRAND DAM
- DAM
  - GRAND SIRE
    - GREAT GRAND SIRE
    - GREAT GRAND DAM
  - GRAND DAM
    - GREAT GRAND SIRE
    - GREAT GRAND DAM

MEDICAL INFORMATION

INJURY OR ILLNESS

DATE	DESCRIPTION OR NATURE OF ILLNESS	TREATMENT

PARASITE CONTROL

DATE	METHOD OR DEWORMER	DATE	METHOD OR DEWORMER

TESTING RECORD

DATE	TEST PERFORMED (CAE, CL, TB…)	RESULT	DATE	TEST PERFORMED (CAE, CL, TB…)	RESULT

VACCINATION & SUPPLEMENT RECORD

DATE	TARGET DISEASE	DRUG OR SUPPLEMENT USED	DOSAGE	RESULTS

DOE'S KIDDING RECORD

DOE'S NAME:

DATE BREED	KIDDING DATE	# OF KIDS	SEX D/B	NAME OF KID	SIRE OF KID	WEIGHT	TATTOO

BUCK'S RECORD OF PROGENY

DOE'S NAME:

YEAR	BRED TO	KIDS	DOE/BUCK

GOAT RECORD

GOAT'S NAME:		IDENTIFICATION:	
BREED:	DATE OF BIRTH:		DATE OF WEANED:

WEIGHT (POUNDS)

BIRTH	JAN	FEB	MAR	APR	MAY	JUN	JUL	AUG	SEP	OCT	NOV	DEC	FINAL

FEED RECORD

	JAN	FEB	MAR	APR	MAY	JUN	JUL	AUG	SEP	OCT	NOV	DEC	TOTAL
GRAIN													
GRAIN													
PASTURE													

MILK PRODUCTION

DOE'S NAME:		IDENTIFICATION:	
BREED:	DATE OF BIRTH:	KIDDING DATE:	

JANUARY		AVERAGE LBS / DAY X 31 DAYS =		LBS
FEBRUARY		AVERAGE LBS / DAY X 31 DAYS =		LBS
MARCH		AVERAGE LBS / DAY X 31 DAYS =		LBS
APRIL		AVERAGE LBS / DAY X 31 DAYS =		LBS
MAY		AVERAGE LBS / DAY X 31 DAYS =		LBS
JUNE		AVERAGE LBS / DAY X 31 DAYS =		LBS
JULY		AVERAGE LBS / DAY X 31 DAYS =		LBS
AUGUST		AVERAGE LBS / DAY X 31 DAYS =		LBS
SEPTEMBER		AVERAGE LBS / DAY X 31 DAYS =		LBS
OCTOBER		AVERAGE LBS / DAY X 31 DAYS =		LBS
NOVEMBER		AVERAGE LBS / DAY X 31 DAYS =		LBS
DECEMBER		AVERAGE LBS / DAY X 31 DAYS =		LBS
YEARLY TOTAL MILK PRODUCED =				LBS

TOTAL VALUE OF MILK PRODUCED FOR THE YEAR

	LBS X $		VALUE PER LBS =	

GOAT INFORMATION

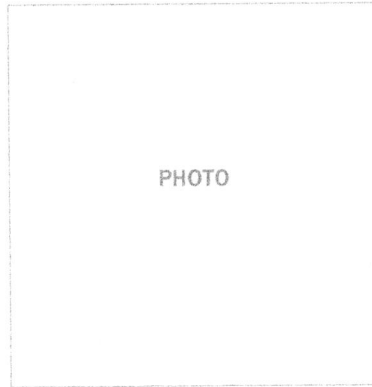

PHOTO

NAME	☐ BUCK	☐ DOE
BREED	BIRTH DATE:	

DATE ACQUIRED:	HOW ACQUIRED: ☐ BORN ON FARM ☐ PURCHASED ☐ LEASED

COLORS / IDENTIFYING MARKS:

PURPOSE:	☐ MILK	☐ MEAT	☐ PET	☐ OTHER

PEDIGREE CHART

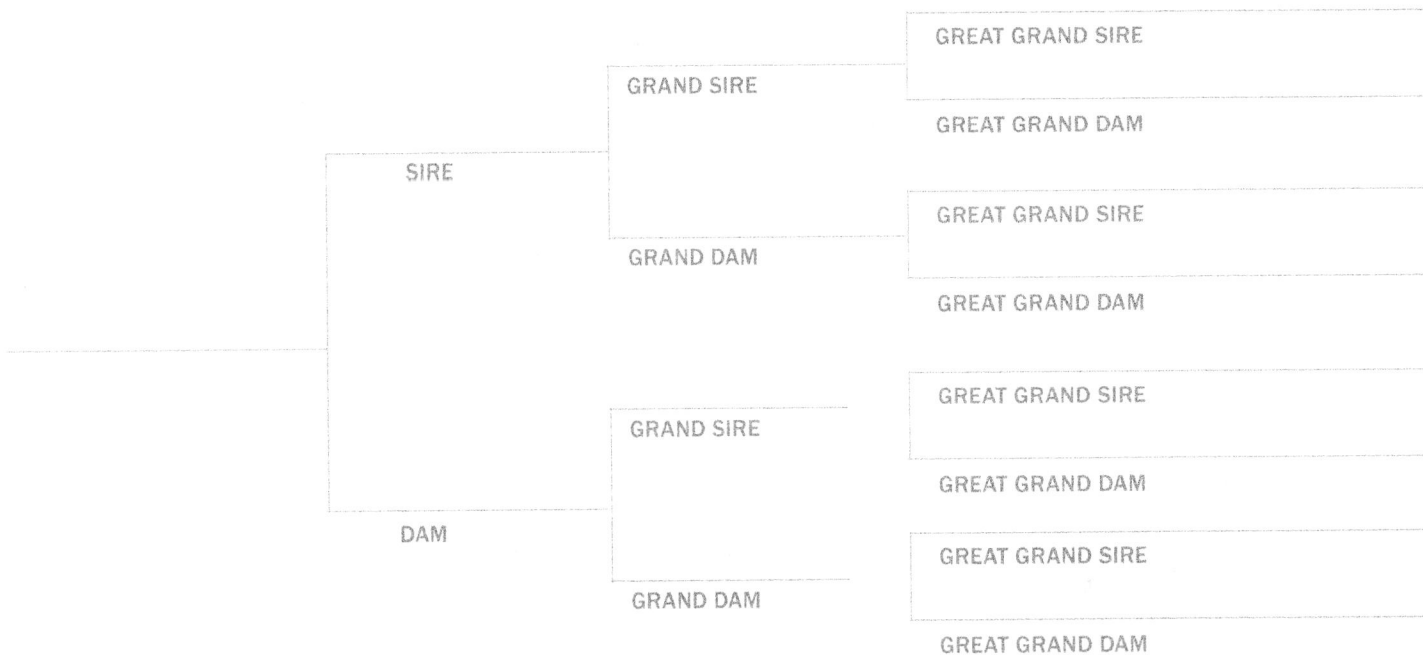

SIRE

- GRAND SIRE
  - GREAT GRAND SIRE
  - GREAT GRAND DAM
- GRAND DAM
  - GREAT GRAND SIRE
  - GREAT GRAND DAM

DAM

- GRAND SIRE
  - GREAT GRAND SIRE
  - GREAT GRAND DAM
- GRAND DAM
  - GREAT GRAND SIRE
  - GREAT GRAND DAM

MEDICAL INFORMATION

INJURY OR ILLNESS

DATE	DESCRIPTION OR NATURE OF ILLNESS	TREATMENT

PARASITE CONTROL

DATE	METHOD OR DEWORMER	DATE	METHOD OR DEWORMER

TESTING RECORD

DATE	TEST PERFORMED (CAE, CL, TB...)	RESULT	DATE	TEST PERFORMED (CAE, CL, TB...)	RESULT

VACCINATION & SUPPLEMENT RECORD

DATE	TARGET DISEASE	DRUG OR SUPPLEMENT USED	DOSAGE	RESULTS

DOE'S KIDDING RECORD

DOE'S NAME:	

DATE BREED	KIDDING DATE	# OF KIDS	SEX D/B	NAME OF KID	SIRE OF KID	WEIGHT	TATTOO

BUCK'S RECORD OF PROGENY

DOE'S NAME:

YEAR	BRED TO	KIDS	DOE/BUCK

GOAT RECORD

GOAT'S NAME:		IDENTIFICATION:
BREED:	DATE OF BIRTH:	DATE OF WEANED:

WEIGHT (POUNDS)

BIRTH	JAN	FEB	MAR	APR	MAY	JUN	JUL	AUG	SEP	OCT	NOV	DEC	FINAL

FEED RECORD

	JAN	FEB	MAR	APR	MAY	JUN	JUL	AUG	SEP	OCT	NOV	DEC	TOTAL
GRAIN													
GRAIN													
PASTURE													

MILK PRODUCTION

DOE'S NAME:		IDENTIFICATION:	
BREED:	DATE OF BIRTH:	KIDDING DATE:	

JANUARY		AVERAGE LBS / DAY X 31 DAYS =		LBS
FEBRUARY		AVERAGE LBS / DAY X 31 DAYS =		LBS
MARCH		AVERAGE LBS / DAY X 31 DAYS =		LBS
APRIL		AVERAGE LBS / DAY X 31 DAYS =		LBS
MAY		AVERAGE LBS / DAY X 31 DAYS =		LBS
JUNE		AVERAGE LBS / DAY X 31 DAYS =		LBS
JULY		AVERAGE LBS / DAY X 31 DAYS =		LBS
AUGUST		AVERAGE LBS / DAY X 31 DAYS =		LBS
SEPTEMBER		AVERAGE LBS / DAY X 31 DAYS =		LBS
OCTOBER		AVERAGE LBS / DAY X 31 DAYS =		LBS
NOVEMBER		AVERAGE LBS / DAY X 31 DAYS =		LBS
DECEMBER		AVERAGE LBS / DAY X 31 DAYS =		LBS
YEARLY TOTAL MILK PRODUCED =				LBS

TOTAL VALUE OF MILK PRODUCED FOR THE YEAR

LBS X $		VALUE PER LBS =

GOAT INFORMATION

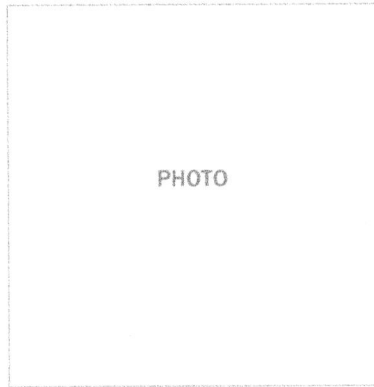

PHOTO

NAME	☐ BUCK	☐ DOE
BREED	BIRTH DATE:	
DATE ACQUIRED:	HOW ACQUIRED: ☐ BORN ON FARM ☐ PURCHASED ☐ LEASED	
COLORS / IDENTIFYING MARKS:		

PURPOSE:	☐ MILK	☐ MEAT	☐ PET	☐ OTHER

PEDIGREE CHART

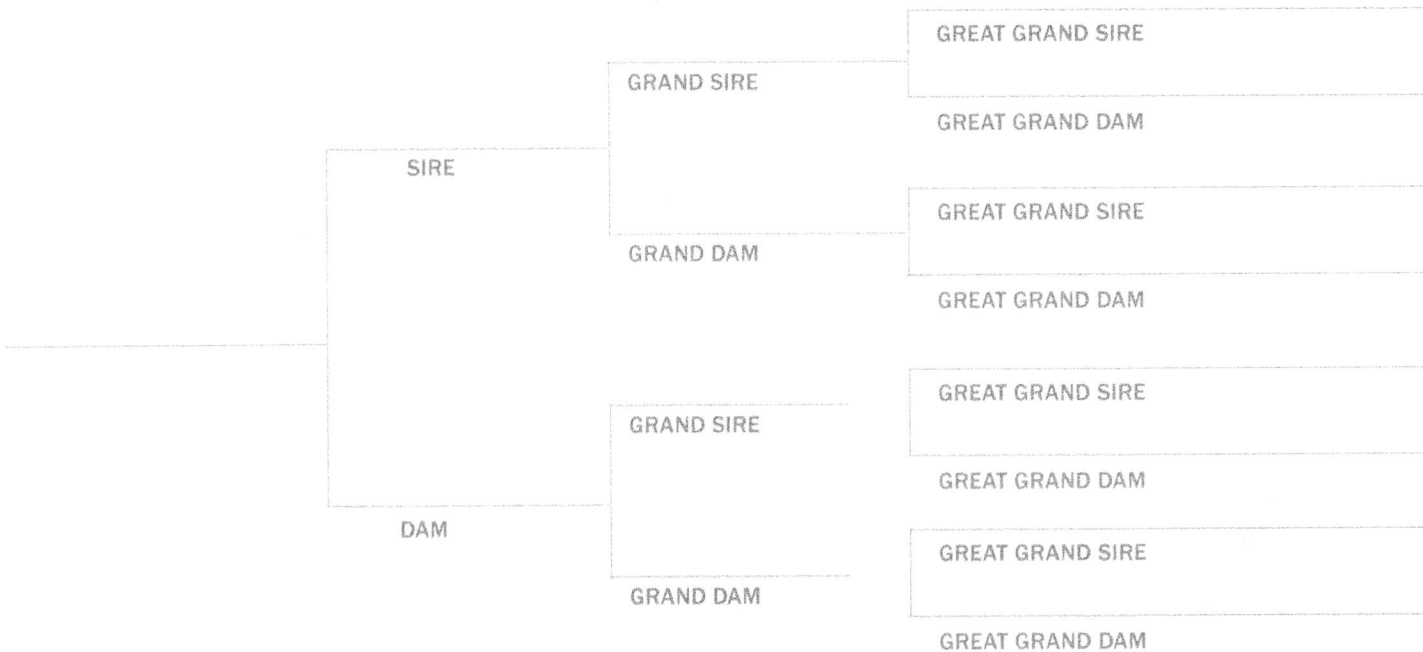

- SIRE
  - GRAND SIRE
    - GREAT GRAND SIRE
    - GREAT GRAND DAM
  - GRAND DAM
    - GREAT GRAND SIRE
    - GREAT GRAND DAM
- DAM
  - GRAND SIRE
    - GREAT GRAND SIRE
    - GREAT GRAND DAM
  - GRAND DAM
    - GREAT GRAND SIRE
    - GREAT GRAND DAM

MEDICAL INFORMATION

INJURY OR ILLNESS

DATE	DESCRIPTION OR NATURE OF ILLNESS	TREATMENT

PARASITE CONTROL

DATE	METHOD OR DEWORMER	DATE	METHOD OR DEWORMER

TESTING RECORD

DATE	TEST PERFORMED (CAE, CL, TB...)	RESULT	DATE	TEST PERFORMED (CAE, CL, TB...)	RESULT

VACCINATION & SUPPLEMENT RECORD

DATE	TARGET DISEASE	DRUG OR SUPPLEMENT USED	DOSAGE	RESULTS

DOE'S KIDDING RECORD

DOE'S NAME:

DATE BREED	KIDDING DATE	# OF KIDS	SEX D/B	NAME OF KID	SIRE OF KID	WEIGHT	TATTOO

BUCK'S RECORD OF PROGENY

DOE'S NAME:

YEAR	BRED TO	KIDS	DOE/BUCK

GOAT RECORD

GOAT'S NAME:		IDENTIFICATION:	
BREED:	DATE OF BIRTH:		DATE OF WEANED:

WEIGHT (POUNDS)

BIRTH	JAN	FEB	MAR	APR	MAY	JUN	JUL	AUG	SEP	OCT	NOV	DEC	FINAL

FEED RECORD

	JAN	FEB	MAR	APR	MAY	JUN	JUL	AUG	SEP	OCT	NOV	DEC	TOTAL
GRAIN													
GRAIN													
PASTURE													

MILK PRODUCTION

DOE'S NAME:		IDENTIFICATION:	
BREED:	DATE OF BIRTH:	KIDDING DATE:	

JANUARY		AVERAGE LBS / DAY X 31 DAYS =		LBS
FEBRUARY		AVERAGE LBS / DAY X 31 DAYS =		LBS
MARCH		AVERAGE LBS / DAY X 31 DAYS =		LBS
APRIL		AVERAGE LBS / DAY X 31 DAYS =		LBS
MAY		AVERAGE LBS / DAY X 31 DAYS =		LBS
JUNE		AVERAGE LBS / DAY X 31 DAYS =		LBS
JULY		AVERAGE LBS / DAY X 31 DAYS =		LBS
AUGUST		AVERAGE LBS / DAY X 31 DAYS =		LBS
SEPTEMBER		AVERAGE LBS / DAY X 31 DAYS =		LBS
OCTOBER		AVERAGE LBS / DAY X 31 DAYS =		LBS
NOVEMBER		AVERAGE LBS / DAY X 31 DAYS =		LBS
DECEMBER		AVERAGE LBS / DAY X 31 DAYS =		LBS
YEARLY TOTAL MILK PRODUCED =				LBS

TOTAL VALUE OF MILK PRODUCED FOR THE YEAR

	LBS X $		VALUE PER LBS =	

GOAT INFORMATION

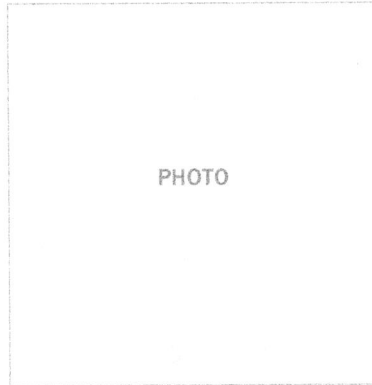

PHOTO

NAME	☐ BUCK	☐ DOE
BREED	BIRTH DATE:	

DATE ACQUIRED: | HOW ACQUIRED: ☐ BORN ON FARM ☐ PURCHASED ☐ LEASED

COLORS / IDENTIFYING MARKS:

PURPOSE: ☐ MILK ☐ MEAT ☐ PET ☐ OTHER

PEDIGREE CHART

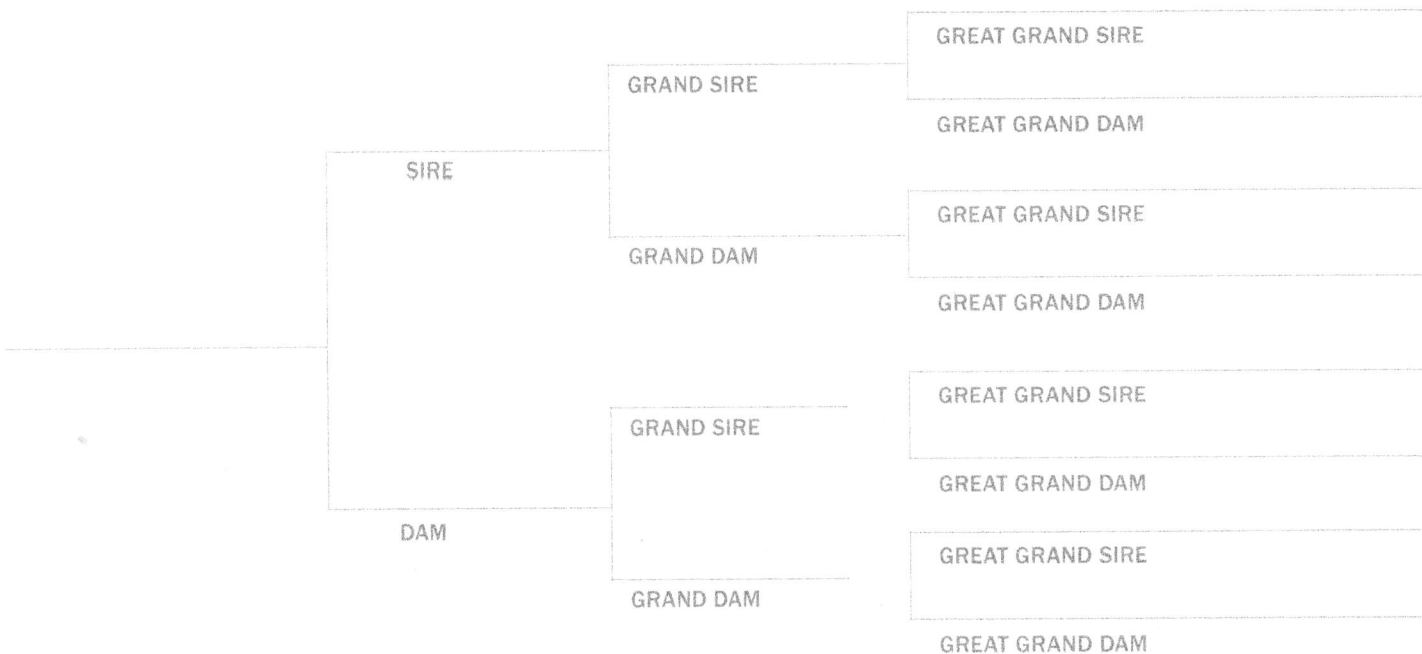

SIRE

GRAND SIRE
- GREAT GRAND SIRE
- GREAT GRAND DAM

GRAND DAM
- GREAT GRAND SIRE
- GREAT GRAND DAM

DAM

GRAND SIRE
- GREAT GRAND SIRE
- GREAT GRAND DAM

GRAND DAM
- GREAT GRAND SIRE
- GREAT GRAND DAM

MEDICAL INFORMATION

INJURY OR ILLNESS

DATE	DESCRIPTION OR NATURE OF ILLNESS	TREATMENT

PARASITE CONTROL

DATE	METHOD OR DEWORMER	DATE	METHOD OR DEWORMER

TESTING RECORD

DATE	TEST PERFORMED (CAE. CL. TB...)	RESULT	DATE	TEST PERFORMED (CAE. CL. TB...)	RESULT

VACCINATION & SUPPLEMENT RECORD

DATE	TARGET DISEASE	DRUG OR SUPPLEMENT USED	DOSAGE	RESULTS

DOE'S KIDDING RECORD

DOE'S NAME:

DATE BREED	KIDDING DATE	# OF KIDS	SEX D/B	NAME OF KID	SIRE OF KID	WEIGHT	TATTOO

BUCK'S RECORD OF PROGENY

DOE'S NAME:

YEAR	BRED TO	KIDS	DOE/BUCK

GOAT RECORD

GOAT'S NAME:	IDENTIFICATION:	
BREED:	DATE OF BIRTH:	DATE OF WEANED:

WEIGHT (POUNDS)

BIRTH	JAN	FEB	MAR	APR	MAY	JUN	JUL	AUG	SEP	OCT	NOV	DEC	FINAL

FEED RECORD

	JAN	FEB	MAR	APR	MAY	JUN	JUL	AUG	SEP	OCT	NOV	DEC	TOTAL
GRAIN													
GRAIN													
PASTURE													

MILK PRODUCTION

DOE'S NAME:		IDENTIFICATION:	
BREED:	DATE OF BIRTH:	KIDDING DATE:	

JANUARY		AVERAGE LBS / DAY X 31 DAYS =		LBS
FEBRUARY		AVERAGE LBS / DAY X 31 DAYS =		LBS
MARCH		AVERAGE LBS / DAY X 31 DAYS =		LBS
APRIL		AVERAGE LBS / DAY X 31 DAYS =		LBS
MAY		AVERAGE LBS / DAY X 31 DAYS =		LBS
JUNE		AVERAGE LBS / DAY X 31 DAYS =		LBS
JULY		AVERAGE LBS / DAY X 31 DAYS =		LBS
AUGUST		AVERAGE LBS / DAY X 31 DAYS =		LBS
SEPTEMBER		AVERAGE LBS / DAY X 31 DAYS =		LBS
OCTOBER		AVERAGE LBS / DAY X 31 DAYS =		LBS
NOVEMBER		AVERAGE LBS / DAY X 31 DAYS =		LBS
DECEMBER		AVERAGE LBS / DAY X 31 DAYS =		LBS
YEARLY TOTAL MILK PRODUCED =			LBS

TOTAL VALUE OF MILK PRODUCED FOR THE YEAR

	LBS X $		VALUE PER LBS =	

GOAT INFORMATION

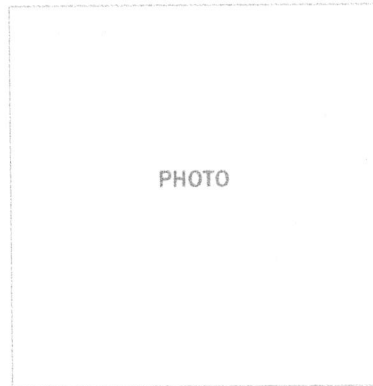

PHOTO

NAME	☐ BUCK	☐ DOE
BREED	BIRTH DATE:	

DATE ACQUIRED: | HOW ACQUIRED: ☐ BORN ON FARM ☐ PURCHASED ☐ LEASED

COLORS / IDENTIFYING MARKS:

PURPOSE: | ☐ MILK | ☐ MEAT | ☐ PET | ☐ OTHER

PEDIGREE CHART

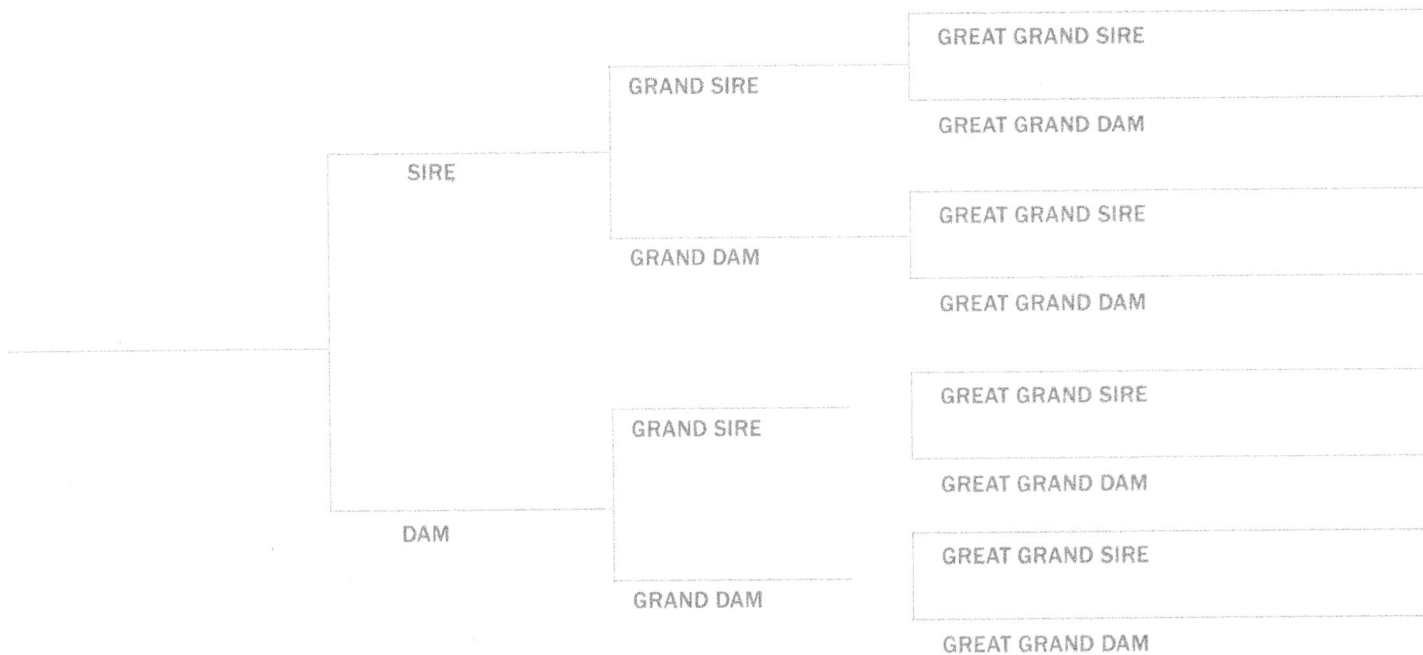

- SIRE
  - GRAND SIRE
    - GREAT GRAND SIRE
    - GREAT GRAND DAM
  - GRAND DAM
    - GREAT GRAND SIRE
    - GREAT GRAND DAM
- DAM
  - GRAND SIRE
    - GREAT GRAND SIRE
    - GREAT GRAND DAM
  - GRAND DAM
    - GREAT GRAND SIRE
    - GREAT GRAND DAM

MEDICAL INFORMATION

INJURY OR ILLNESS

DATE	DESCRIPTION OR NATURE OF ILLNESS	TREATMENT

PARASITE CONTROL

DATE	METHOD OR DEWORMER	DATE	METHOD OR DEWORMER

TESTING RECORD

DATE	TEST PERFORMED (CAE, CL, TB...)	RESULT	DATE	TEST PERFORMED (CAE, CL, TB...)	RESULT

VACCINATION & SUPPLEMENT RECORD

DATE	TARGET DISEASE	DRUG OR SUPPLEMENT USED	DOSAGE	RESULTS

DOE'S KIDDING RECORD

DOE'S NAME:

DATE BREED	KIDDING DATE	# OF KIDS	SEX D/B	NAME OF KID	SIRE OF KID	WEIGHT	TATTOO

BUCK'S RECORD OF PROGENY

DOE'S NAME:

YEAR	BRED TO	KIDS	DOE/BUCK

GOAT RECORD

GOAT'S NAME:		IDENTIFICATION:	
BREED:	DATE OF BIRTH:		DATE OF WEANED:

WEIGHT (POUNDS)

BIRTH	JAN	FEB	MAR	APR	MAY	JUN	JUL	AUG	SEP	OCT	NOV	DEC	FINAL

FEED RECORD

	JAN	FEB	MAR	APR	MAY	JUN	JUL	AUG	SEP	OCT	NOV	DEC	TOTAL
GRAIN													
GRAIN													
PASTURE													

MILK PRODUCTION

DOE'S NAME:		IDENTIFICATION:	
BREED:	DATE OF BIRTH:	KIDDING DATE:	

JANUARY		AVERAGE LBS / DAY X 31 DAYS =		LBS
FEBRUARY		AVERAGE LBS / DAY X 31 DAYS =		LBS
MARCH		AVERAGE LBS / DAY X 31 DAYS =		LBS
APRIL		AVERAGE LBS / DAY X 31 DAYS =		LBS
MAY		AVERAGE LBS / DAY X 31 DAYS =		LBS
JUNE		AVERAGE LBS / DAY X 31 DAYS =		LBS
JULY		AVERAGE LBS / DAY X 31 DAYS =		LBS
AUGUST		AVERAGE LBS / DAY X 31 DAYS =		LBS
SEPTEMBER		AVERAGE LBS / DAY X 31 DAYS =		LBS
OCTOBER		AVERAGE LBS / DAY X 31 DAYS =		LBS
NOVEMBER		AVERAGE LBS / DAY X 31 DAYS =		LBS
DECEMBER		AVERAGE LBS / DAY X 31 DAYS =		LBS
YEARLY TOTAL MILK PRODUCED =				LBS

TOTAL VALUE OF MILK PRODUCED FOR THE YEAR

	LBS X $		VALUE PER LBS =	

GOAT INFORMATION

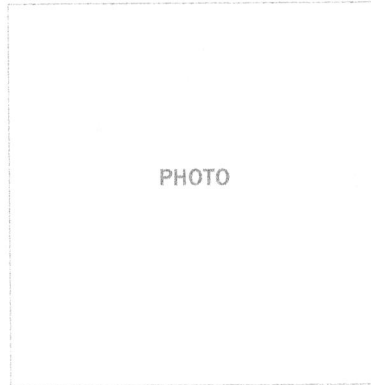

PHOTO

NAME		☐ BUCK	☐ DOE
BREED		BIRTH DATE:	

DATE ACQUIRED:	HOW ACQUIRED: ☐ BORN ON FARM ☐ PURCHASED ☐ LEASED

COLORS / IDENTIFYING MARKS:

PURPOSE:	☐ MILK	☐ MEAT	☐ PET	☐ OTHER

PEDIGREE CHART

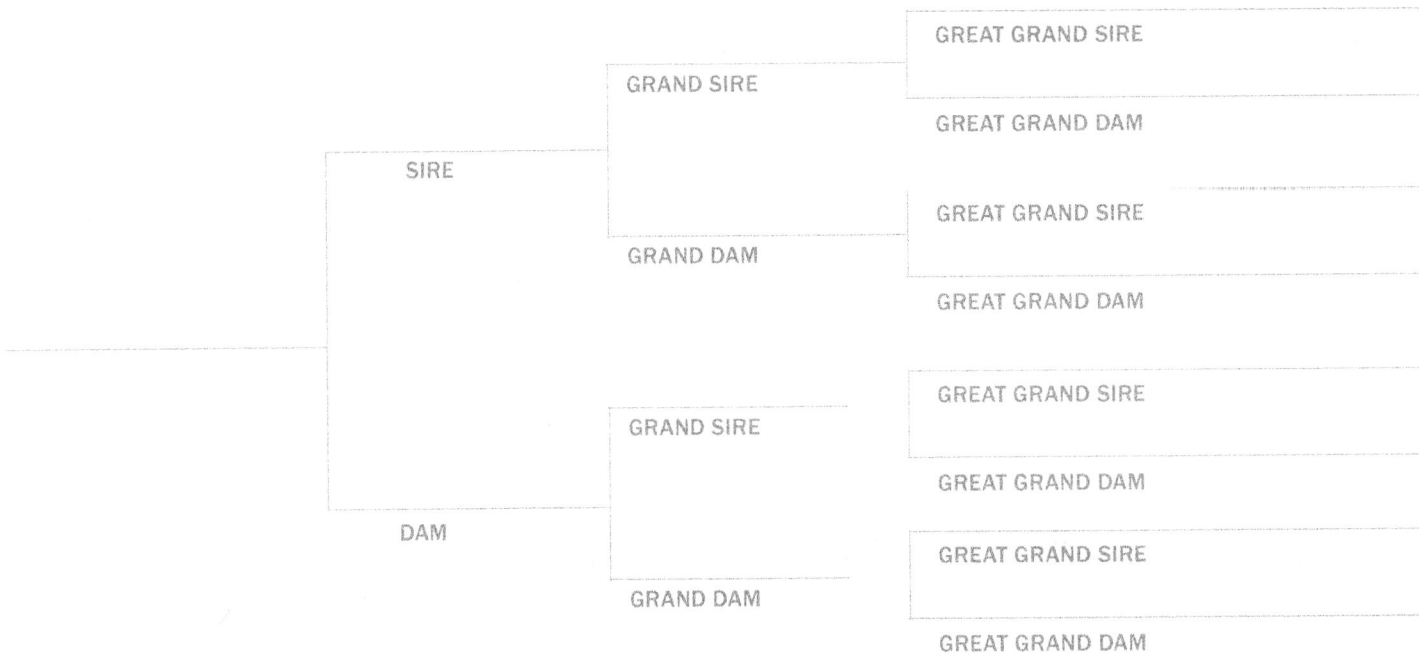

SIRE

- GRAND SIRE
  - GREAT GRAND SIRE
  - GREAT GRAND DAM
- GRAND DAM
  - GREAT GRAND SIRE
  - GREAT GRAND DAM

DAM

- GRAND SIRE
  - GREAT GRAND SIRE
  - GREAT GRAND DAM
- GRAND DAM
  - GREAT GRAND SIRE
  - GREAT GRAND DAM

MEDICAL INFORMATION

INJURY OR ILLNESS

DATE	DESCRIPTION OR NATURE OF ILLNESS	TREATMENT

PARASITE CONTROL

DATE	METHOD OR DEWORMER	DATE	METHOD OR DEWORMER

TESTING RECORD

DATE	TEST PERFORMED (CAE, CL, TB...)	RESULT	DATE	TEST PERFORMED (CAE, CL, TB...)	RESULT

VACCINATION & SUPPLEMENT RECORD

DATE	TARGET DISEASE	DRUG OR SUPPLEMENT USED	DOSAGE	RESULTS

DOE'S KIDDING RECORD

DOE'S NAME:

DATE BREED	KIDDING DATE	# OF KIDS	SEX D/B	NAME OF KID	SIRE OF KID	WEIGHT	TATTOO

BUCK'S RECORD OF PROGENY

DOE'S NAME:

YEAR	BRED TO	KIDS	DOE/BUCK

GOAT RECORD

GOAT'S NAME:		IDENTIFICATION:

BREED:		DATE OF BIRTH:	DATE OF WEANED:

WEIGHT (POUNDS)

BIRTH	JAN	FEB	MAR	APR	MAY	JUN	JUL	AUG	SEP	OCT	NOV	DEC	FINAL

FEED RECORD

	JAN	FEB	MAR	APR	MAY	JUN	JUL	AUG	SEP	OCT	NOV	DEC	TOTAL
GRAIN													
GRAIN													
PASTURE													

MILK PRODUCTION

DOE'S NAME: IDENTIFICATION:

BREED: DATE OF BIRTH: KIDDING DATE:

JANUARY		AVERAGE LBS / DAY X 31 DAYS =		LBS
FEBRUARY		AVERAGE LBS / DAY X 31 DAYS =		LBS
MARCH		AVERAGE LBS / DAY X 31 DAYS =		LBS
APRIL		AVERAGE LBS / DAY X 31 DAYS =		LBS
MAY		AVERAGE LBS / DAY X 31 DAYS =		LBS
JUNE		AVERAGE LBS / DAY X 31 DAYS =		LBS
JULY		AVERAGE LBS / DAY X 31 DAYS =		LBS
AUGUST		AVERAGE LBS / DAY X 31 DAYS =		LBS
SEPTEMBER		AVERAGE LBS / DAY X 31 DAYS =		LBS
OCTOBER		AVERAGE LBS / DAY X 31 DAYS =		LBS
NOVEMBER		AVERAGE LBS / DAY X 31 DAYS =		LBS
DECEMBER		AVERAGE LBS / DAY X 31 DAYS =		LBS
YEARLY TOTAL MILK PRODUCED =				LBS

TOTAL VALUE OF MILK PRODUCED FOR THE YEAR

LBS X $		VALUE PER LBS =	

GOAT INFORMATION

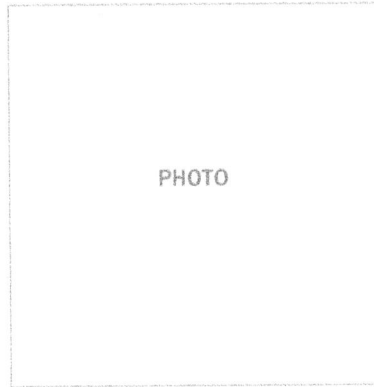

PHOTO

NAME		☐ BUCK	☐ DOE
BREED		BIRTH DATE:	
DATE ACQUIRED:	HOW ACQUIRED: ☐ BORN ON FARM ☐ PURCHASED ☐ LEASED		
COLORS / IDENTIFYING MARKS:			
PURPOSE: ☐ MILK ☐ MEAT ☐ PET ☐ OTHER			

PEDIGREE CHART

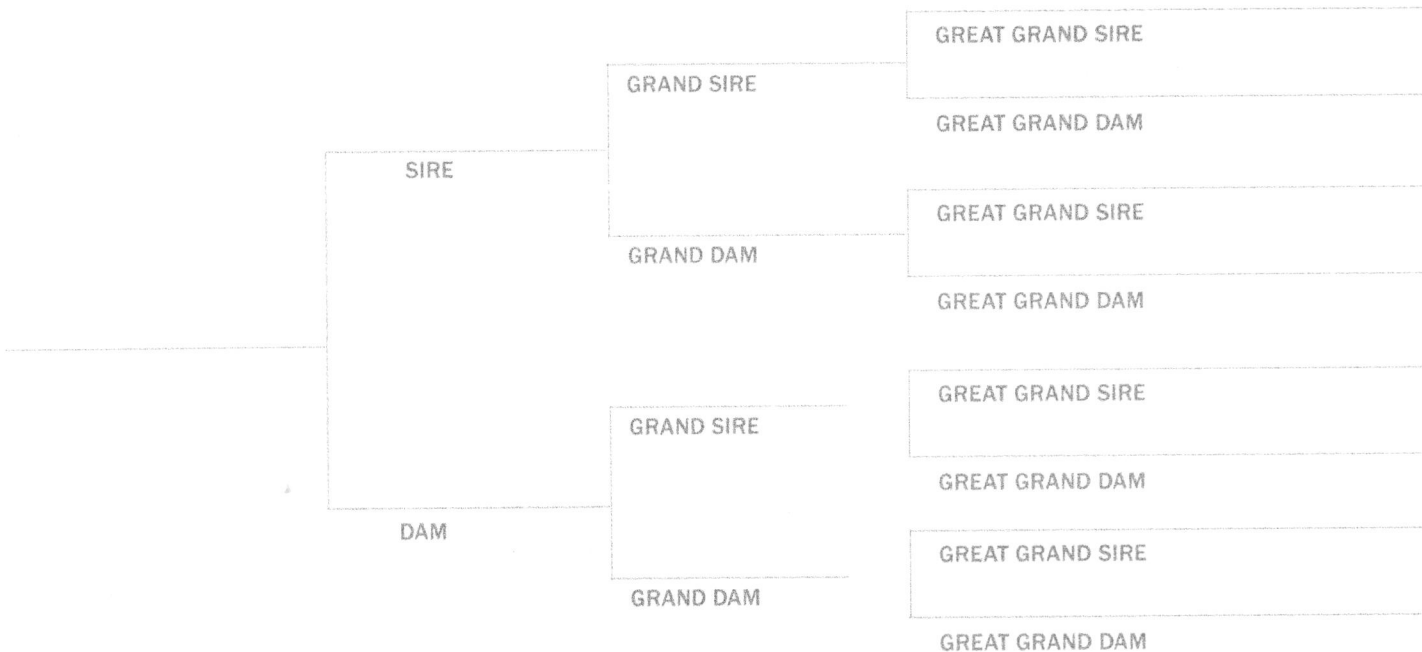

SIRE

DAM

GRAND SIRE

GRAND DAM

GRAND SIRE

GRAND DAM

GREAT GRAND SIRE

GREAT GRAND DAM

GREAT GRAND SIRE

GREAT GRAND DAM

GREAT GRAND SIRE

GREAT GRAND DAM

GREAT GRAND SIRE

GREAT GRAND DAM

MEDICAL INFORMATION

INJURY OR ILLNESS

DATE	DESCRIPTION OR NATURE OF ILLNESS	TREATMENT

PARASITE CONTROL

DATE	METHOD OR DEWORMER	DATE	METHOD OR DEWORMER

TESTING RECORD

DATE	TEST PERFORMED (CAE, CL, TB...)	RESULT	DATE	TEST PERFORMED (CAE, CL, TB...)	RESULT

VACCINATION & SUPPLEMENT RECORD

DATE	TARGET DISEASE	DRUG OR SUPPLEMENT USED	DOSAGE	RESULTS

DOE'S KIDDING RECORD

DOE'S NAME:

DATE BREED	KIDDING DATE	# OF KIDS	SEX D/B	NAME OF KID	SIRE OF KID	WEIGHT	TATTOO

BUCK'S RECORD OF PROGENY

DOE'S NAME:

YEAR	BRED TO	KIDS	DOE/BUCK

GOAT RECORD

GOAT'S NAME:		IDENTIFICATION:	
BREED:	DATE OF BIRTH:	DATE OF WEANED:	

WEIGHT (POUNDS)

BIRTH	JAN	FEB	MAR	APR	MAY	JUN	JUL	AUG	SEP	OCT	NOV	DEC	FINAL

FEED RECORD

	JAN	FEB	MAR	APR	MAY	JUN	JUL	AUG	SEP	OCT	NOV	DEC	TOTAL
GRAIN													
GRAIN													
PASTURE													

MILK PRODUCTION

DOE'S NAME:		IDENTIFICATION:	
BREED:	DATE OF BIRTH:	KIDDING DATE:	

JANUARY		AVERAGE LBS / DAY X 31 DAYS =		LBS
FEBRUARY		AVERAGE LBS / DAY X 31 DAYS =		LBS
MARCH		AVERAGE LBS / DAY X 31 DAYS =		LBS
APRIL		AVERAGE LBS / DAY X 31 DAYS =		LBS
MAY		AVERAGE LBS / DAY X 31 DAYS =		LBS
JUNE		AVERAGE LBS / DAY X 31 DAYS =		LBS
JULY		AVERAGE LBS / DAY X 31 DAYS =		LBS
AUGUST		AVERAGE LBS / DAY X 31 DAYS =		LBS
SEPTEMBER		AVERAGE LBS / DAY X 31 DAYS =		LBS
OCTOBER		AVERAGE LBS / DAY X 31 DAYS =		LBS
NOVEMBER		AVERAGE LBS / DAY X 31 DAYS =		LBS
DECEMBER		AVERAGE LBS / DAY X 31 DAYS =		LBS
YEARLY TOTAL MILK PRODUCED =				LBS

TOTAL VALUE OF MILK PRODUCED FOR THE YEAR

	LBS X $		VALUE PER LBS =	

GOAT INFORMATION

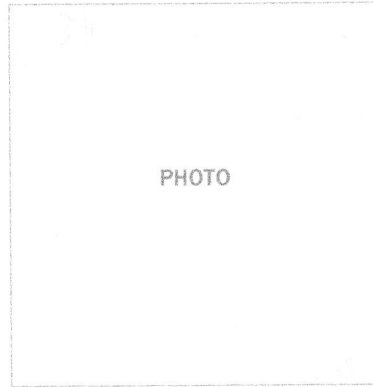

PHOTO

NAME		☐ BUCK	☐ DOE
BREED		BIRTH DATE:	
DATE ACQUIRED:	HOW ACQUIRED: ☐ BORN ON FARM ☐ PURCHASED ☐ LEASED		
COLORS / IDENTIFYING MARKS:			
PURPOSE: ☐ MILK ☐ MEAT ☐ PET ☐ OTHER			

PEDIGREE CHART

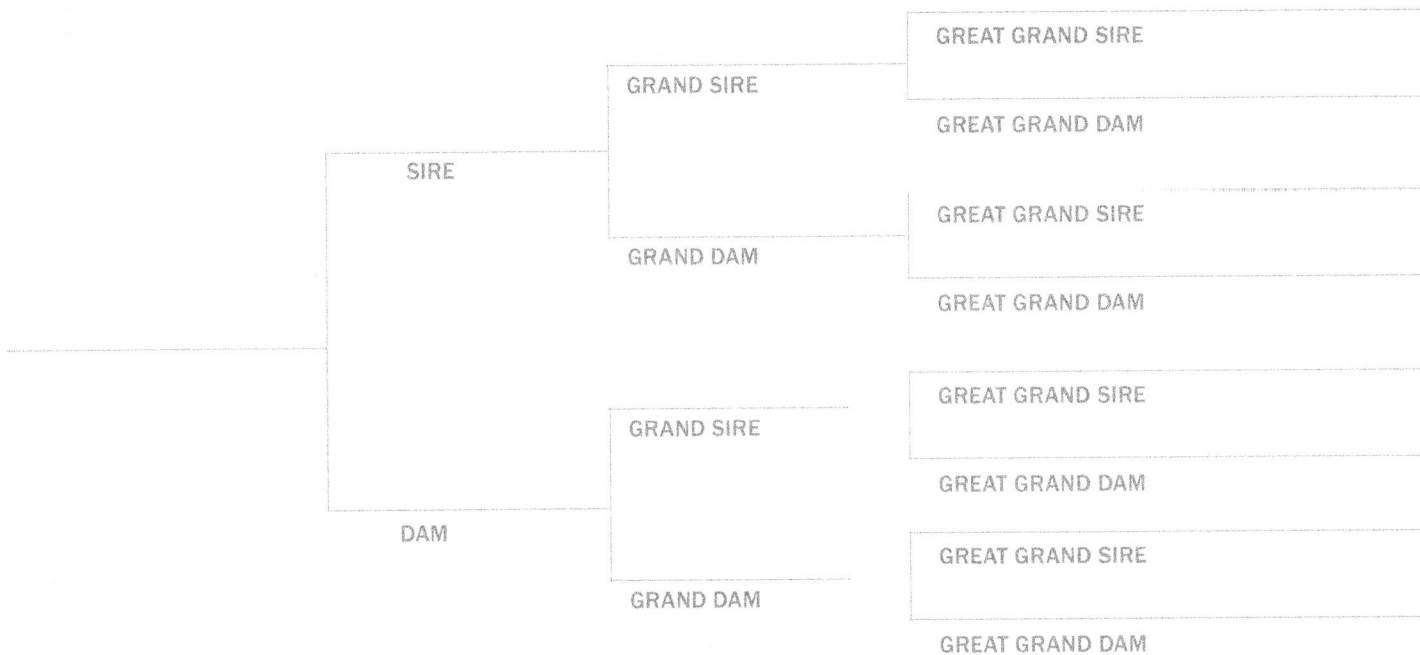

SIRE

GRAND SIRE

GREAT GRAND SIRE

GREAT GRAND DAM

GRAND DAM

GREAT GRAND SIRE

GREAT GRAND DAM

DAM

GRAND SIRE

GREAT GRAND SIRE

GREAT GRAND DAM

GRAND DAM

GREAT GRAND SIRE

GREAT GRAND DAM

MEDICAL INFORMATION

INJURY OR ILLNESS

DATE	DESCRIPTION OR NATURE OF ILLNESS	TREATMENT

PARASITE CONTROL

DATE	METHOD OR DEWORMER	DATE	METHOD OR DEWORMER

TESTING RECORD

DATE	TEST PERFORMED (CAE. CL. TB...)	RESULT	DATE	TEST PERFORMED (CAE. CL. TB...)	RESULT

VACCINATION & SUPPLEMENT RECORD

DATE	TARGET DISEASE	DRUG OR SUPPLEMENT USED	DOSAGE	RESULTS

DOE'S KIDDING RECORD

DOE'S NAME:

DATE BREED	KIDDING DATE	# OF KIDS	SEX D/B	NAME OF KID	SIRE OF KID	WEIGHT	TATTOO

BUCK'S RECORD OF PROGENY

DOE'S NAME:

YEAR	BRED TO	KIDS	DOE/BUCK

GOAT RECORD

GOAT'S NAME:		IDENTIFICATION:	
BREED:	DATE OF BIRTH:	DATE OF WEANED:	

WEIGHT (POUNDS)

BIRTH	JAN	FEB	MAR	APR	MAY	JUN	JUL	AUG	SEP	OCT	NOV	DEC	FINAL

FEED RECORD

	JAN	FEB	MAR	APR	MAY	JUN	JUL	AUG	SEP	OCT	NOV	DEC	TOTAL
GRAIN													
GRAIN													
PASTURE													

MILK PRODUCTION

DOE'S NAME:			IDENTIFICATION:	
BREED:		DATE OF BIRTH:	KIDDING DATE:	

JANUARY		AVERAGE LBS / DAY X 31 DAYS =		LBS
FEBRUARY		AVERAGE LBS / DAY X 31 DAYS =		LBS
MARCH		AVERAGE LBS / DAY X 31 DAYS =		LBS
APRIL		AVERAGE LBS / DAY X 31 DAYS =		LBS
MAY		AVERAGE LBS / DAY X 31 DAYS =		LBS
JUNE		AVERAGE LBS / DAY X 31 DAYS =		LBS
JULY		AVERAGE LBS / DAY X 31 DAYS =		LBS
AUGUST		AVERAGE LBS / DAY X 31 DAYS =		LBS
SEPTEMBER		AVERAGE LBS / DAY X 31 DAYS =		LBS
OCTOBER		AVERAGE LBS / DAY X 31 DAYS =		LBS
NOVEMBER		AVERAGE LBS / DAY X 31 DAYS =		LBS
DECEMBER		AVERAGE LBS / DAY X 31 DAYS =		LBS
YEARLY TOTAL MILK PRODUCED =				LBS

TOTAL VALUE OF MILK PRODUCED FOR THE YEAR

	LBS X $		VALUE PER LBS =	

GOAT INFORMATION

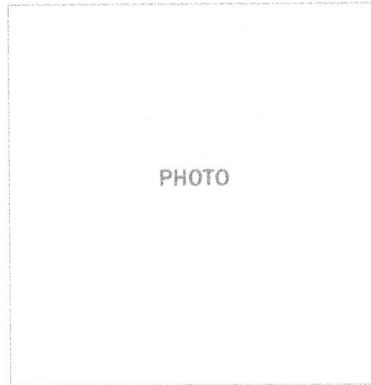

PHOTO

NAME	☐ BUCK	☐ DOE
BREED	BIRTH DATE:	

DATE ACQUIRED:	HOW ACQUIRED: ☐ BORN ON FARM ☐ PURCHASED ☐ LEASED

COLORS / IDENTIFYING MARKS:

PURPOSE:	☐ MILK	☐ MEAT	☐ PET	☐ OTHER

PEDIGREE CHART

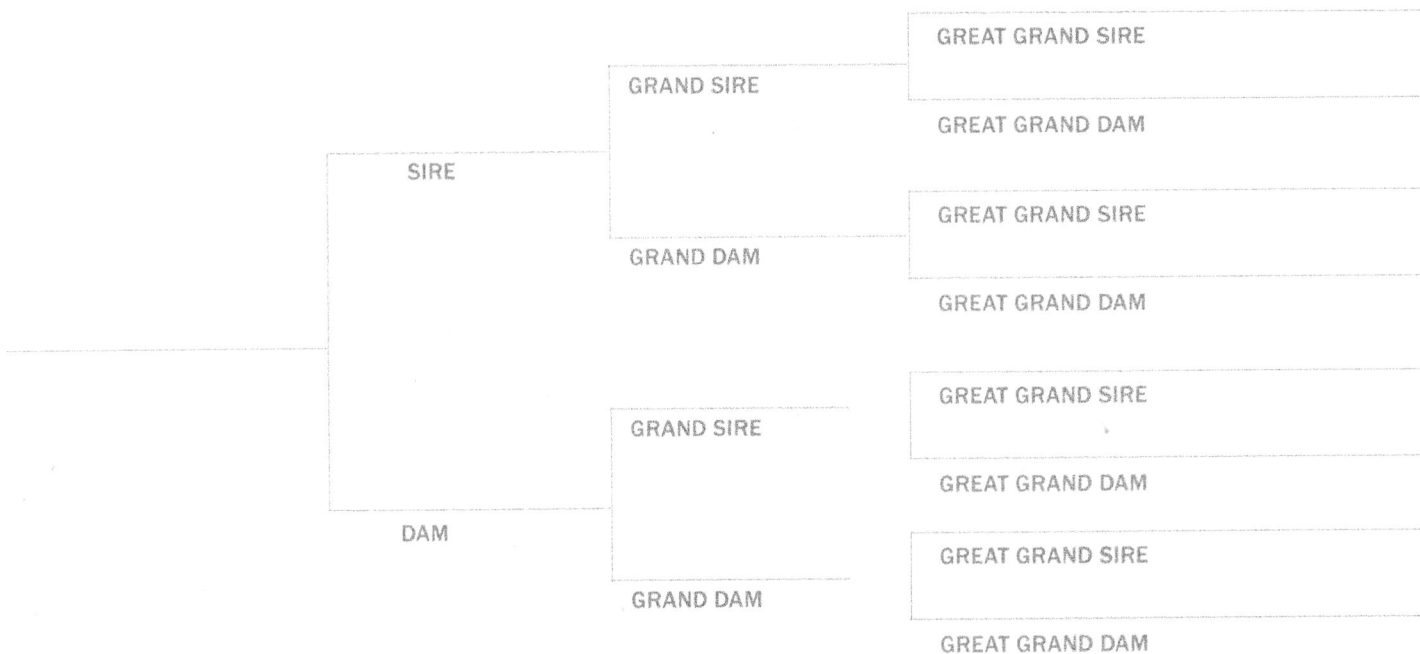

```
                                                    GREAT GRAND SIRE
                                GRAND SIRE
                                                    GREAT GRAND DAM
                SIRE
                                                    GREAT GRAND SIRE
                                GRAND DAM
                                                    GREAT GRAND DAM

                                                    GREAT GRAND SIRE
                                GRAND SIRE
                                                    GREAT GRAND DAM
                DAM
                                                    GREAT GRAND SIRE
                                GRAND DAM
                                                    GREAT GRAND DAM
```

MEDICAL INFORMATION

INJURY OR ILLNESS

DATE	DESCRIPTION OR NATURE OF ILLNESS	TREATMENT

PARASITE CONTROL

DATE	METHOD OR DEWORMER	DATE	METHOD OR DEWORMER

TESTING RECORD

DATE	TEST PERFORMED (CAE, CL, TB...)	RESULT	DATE	TEST PERFORMED (CAE, CL, TB...)	RESULT

VACCINATION & SUPPLEMENT RECORD

DATE	TARGET DISEASE	DRUG OR SUPPLEMENT USED	DOSAGE	RESULTS

DOE'S KIDDING RECORD

DOE'S NAME:

DATE BREED	KIDDING DATE	# OF KIDS	SEX D/B	NAME OF KID	SIRE OF KID	WEIGHT	TATTOO

BUCK'S RECORD OF PROGENY

DOE'S NAME:

YEAR	BRED TO	KIDS	DOE/BUCK

GOAT RECORD

GOAT'S NAME:

IDENTIFICATION:

BREED:

DATE OF BIRTH:

DATE OF WEANED:

WEIGHT (POUNDS)

BIRTH	JAN	FEB	MAR	APR	MAY	JUN	JUL	AUG	SEP	OCT	NOV	DEC	FINAL

FEED RECORD

	JAN	FEB	MAR	APR	MAY	JUN	JUL	AUG	SEP	OCT	NOV	DEC	TOTAL
GRAIN													
GRAIN													
PASTURE													

MILK PRODUCTION

DOE'S NAME:		IDENTIFICATION:	
BREED:	DATE OF BIRTH:	KIDDING DATE:	

JANUARY		AVERAGE LBS / DAY X 31 DAYS =		LBS
FEBRUARY		AVERAGE LBS / DAY X 31 DAYS =		LBS
MARCH		AVERAGE LBS / DAY X 31 DAYS =		LBS
APRIL		AVERAGE LBS / DAY X 31 DAYS =		LBS
MAY		AVERAGE LBS / DAY X 31 DAYS =		LBS
JUNE		AVERAGE LBS / DAY X 31 DAYS =		LBS
JULY		AVERAGE LBS / DAY X 31 DAYS =		LBS
AUGUST		AVERAGE LBS / DAY X 31 DAYS =		LBS
SEPTEMBER		AVERAGE LBS / DAY X 31 DAYS =		LBS
OCTOBER		AVERAGE LBS / DAY X 31 DAYS =		LBS
NOVEMBER		AVERAGE LBS / DAY X 31 DAYS =		LBS
DECEMBER		AVERAGE LBS / DAY X 31 DAYS =		LBS
YEARLY TOTAL MILK PRODUCED =				LBS

TOTAL VALUE OF MILK PRODUCED FOR THE YEAR

	LBS X $		VALUE PER LBS =	

GOAT INFORMATION

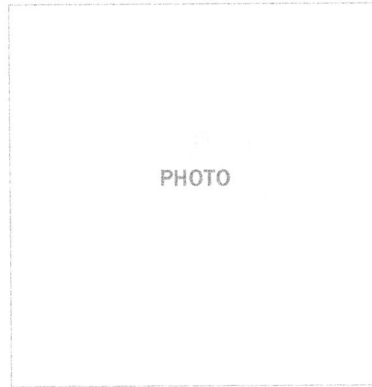

PHOTO

NAME	☐ BUCK	☐ DOE
BREED	BIRTH DATE:	

DATE ACQUIRED:	HOW ACQUIRED: ☐ BORN ON FARM ☐ PURCHASED ☐ LEASED

COLORS / IDENTIFYING MARKS:

PURPOSE:	☐ MILK	☐ MEAT	☐ PET	☐ OTHER

PEDIGREE CHART

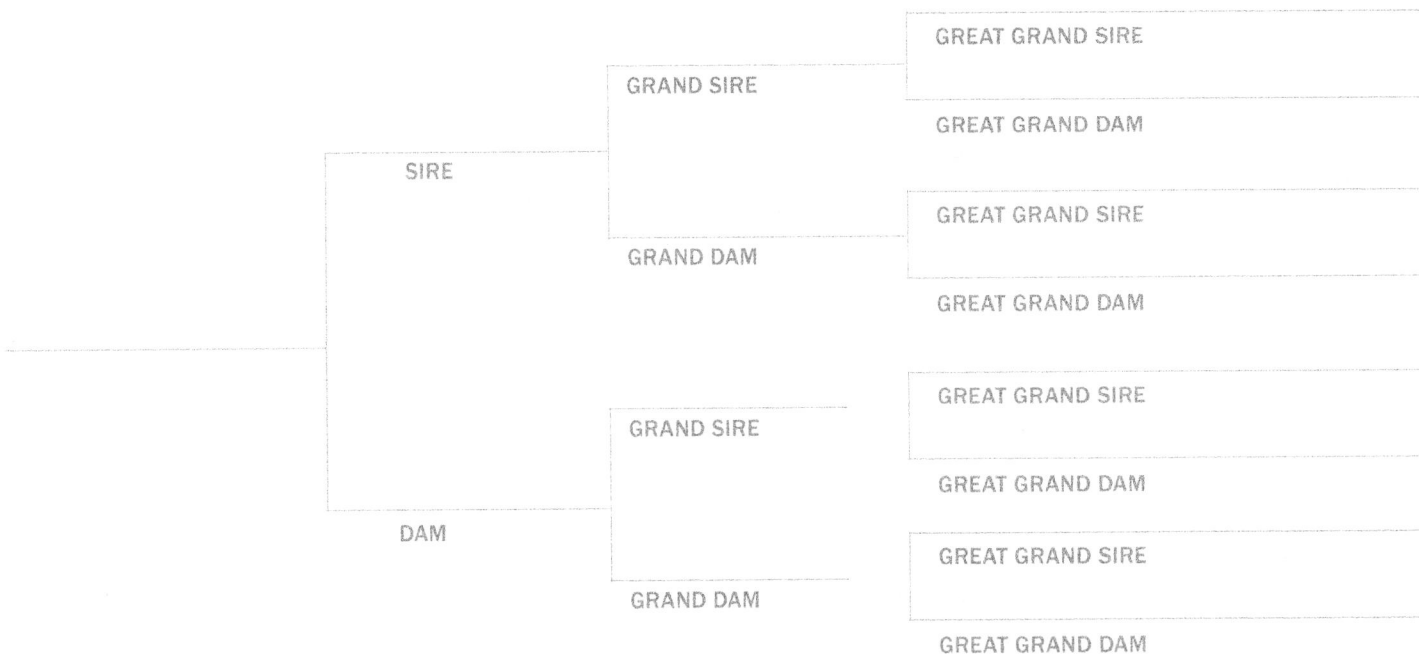

- SIRE
  - GRAND SIRE
    - GREAT GRAND SIRE
    - GREAT GRAND DAM
  - GRAND DAM
    - GREAT GRAND SIRE
    - GREAT GRAND DAM
- DAM
  - GRAND SIRE
    - GREAT GRAND SIRE
    - GREAT GRAND DAM
  - GRAND DAM
    - GREAT GRAND SIRE
    - GREAT GRAND DAM

MEDICAL INFORMATION

INJURY OR ILLNESS

DATE	DESCRIPTION OR NATURE OF ILLNESS	TREATMENT

PARASITE CONTROL

DATE	METHOD OR DEWORMER	DATE	METHOD OR DEWORMER

TESTING RECORD

DATE	TEST PERFORMED (CAE, CL, TB…)	RESULT	DATE	TEST PERFORMED (CAE, CL, TB…)	RESULT

VACCINATION & SUPPLEMENT RECORD

DATE	TARGET DISEASE	DRUG OR SUPPLEMENT USED	DOSAGE	RESULTS

DOE'S KIDDING RECORD

DOE'S NAME:

DATE BREED	KIDDING DATE	# OF KIDS	SEX D/B	NAME OF KID	SIRE OF KID	WEIGHT	TATTOO

BUCK'S RECORD OF PROGENY

DOE'S NAME:

YEAR	BRED TO	KIDS	DOE/BUCK

GOAT RECORD

GOAT'S NAME:		IDENTIFICATION:	
BREED:	DATE OF BIRTH:		DATE OF WEANED:

WEIGHT (POUNDS)

BIRTH	JAN	FEB	MAR	APR	MAY	JUN	JUL	AUG	SEP	OCT	NOV	DEC	FINAL

FEED RECORD

	JAN	FEB	MAR	APR	MAY	JUN	JUL	AUG	SEP	OCT	NOV	DEC	TOTAL
GRAIN													
GRAIN													
PASTURE													

MILK PRODUCTION

DOE'S NAME:		IDENTIFICATION:	
BREED:	DATE OF BIRTH:	KIDDING DATE:	

JANUARY		AVERAGE LBS / DAY X 31 DAYS =		LBS
FEBRUARY		AVERAGE LBS / DAY X 31 DAYS =		LBS
MARCH		AVERAGE LBS / DAY X 31 DAYS =		LBS
APRIL		AVERAGE LBS / DAY X 31 DAYS =		LBS
MAY		AVERAGE LBS / DAY X 31 DAYS =		LBS
JUNE		AVERAGE LBS / DAY X 31 DAYS =		LBS
JULY		AVERAGE LBS / DAY X 31 DAYS =		LBS
AUGUST		AVERAGE LBS / DAY X 31 DAYS =		LBS
SEPTEMBER		AVERAGE LBS / DAY X 31 DAYS =		LBS
OCTOBER		AVERAGE LBS / DAY X 31 DAYS =		LBS
NOVEMBER		AVERAGE LBS / DAY X 31 DAYS =		LBS
DECEMBER		AVERAGE LBS / DAY X 31 DAYS =		LBS
YEARLY TOTAL MILK PRODUCED =				LBS

TOTAL VALUE OF MILK PRODUCED FOR THE YEAR

	LBS X $		VALUE PER LBS =	

GOAT INFORMATION

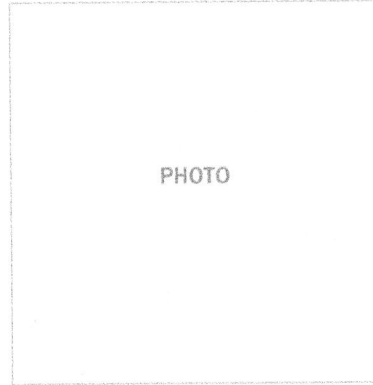

PHOTO

NAME	☐ BUCK	☐ DOE
BREED	BIRTH DATE:	

DATE ACQUIRED: | HOW ACQUIRED: ☐ BORN ON FARM ☐ PURCHASED ☐ LEASED

COLORS / IDENTIFYING MARKS:

PURPOSE: ☐ MILK ☐ MEAT ☐ PET ☐ OTHER

PEDIGREE CHART

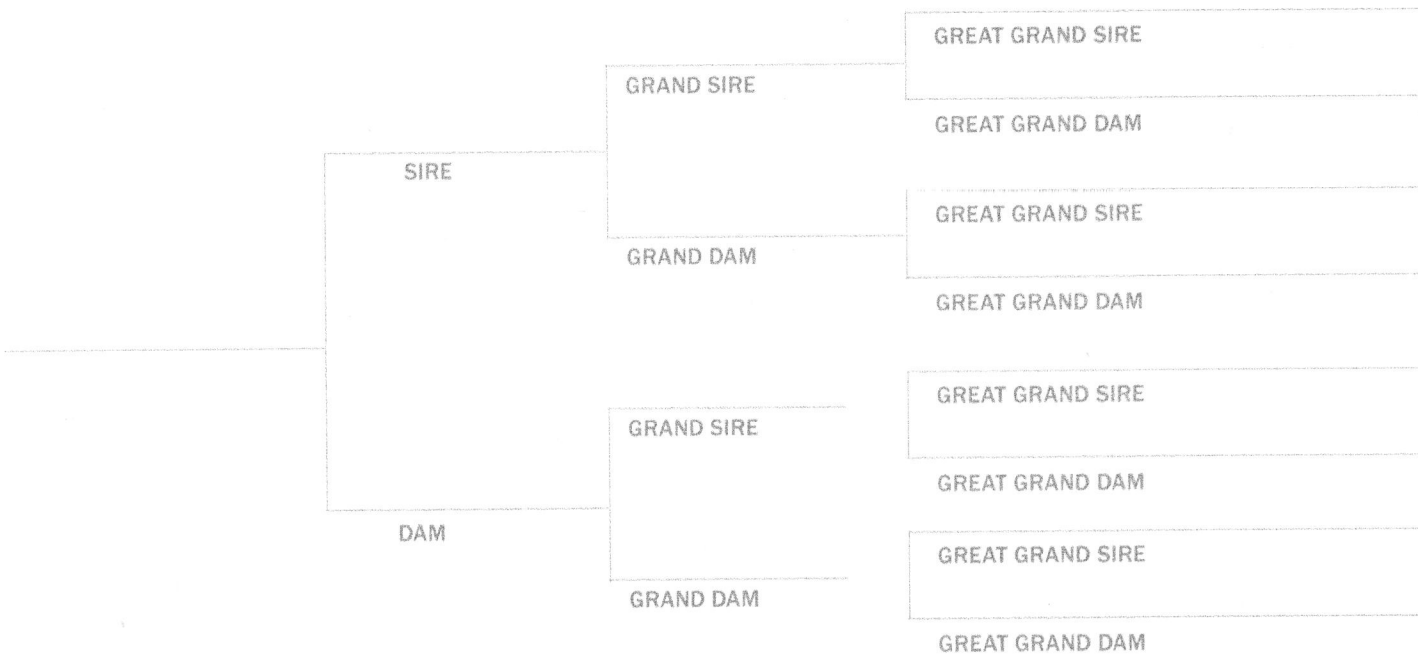

SIRE

GRAND SIRE

GREAT GRAND SIRE

GREAT GRAND DAM

GRAND DAM

GREAT GRAND SIRE

GREAT GRAND DAM

DAM

GRAND SIRE

GREAT GRAND SIRE

GREAT GRAND DAM

GRAND DAM

GREAT GRAND SIRE

GREAT GRAND DAM

MEDICAL INFORMATION

INJURY OR ILLNESS

DATE	DESCRIPTION OR NATURE OF ILLNESS	TREATMENT

PARASITE CONTROL

DATE	METHOD OR DEWORMER	DATE	METHOD OR DEWORMER

TESTING RECORD

DATE	TEST PERFORMED (CAE. CL, TB...)	RESULT	DATE	TEST PERFORMED (CAE, CL, TB...)	RESULT

VACCINATION & SUPPLEMENT RECORD

DATE	TARGET DISEASE	DRUG OR SUPPLEMENT USED	DOSAGE	RESULTS

DOE'S KIDDING RECORD

DOE'S NAME:

DATE BREED	KIDDING DATE	# OF KIDS	SEX D/B	NAME OF KID	SIRE OF KID	WEIGHT	TATTOO

BUCK'S RECORD OF PROGENY

DOE'S NAME:

YEAR	BRED TO	KIDS	DOE/BUCK

GOAT RECORD

GOAT'S NAME:		IDENTIFICATION:	
BREED:	DATE OF BIRTH:		DATE OF WEANED:

WEIGHT (POUNDS)

BIRTH	JAN	FEB	MAR	APR	MAY	JUN	JUL	AUG	SEP	OCT	NOV	DEC	FINAL

FEED RECORD

	JAN	FEB	MAR	APR	MAY	JUN	JUL	AUG	SEP	OCT	NOV	DEC	TOTAL
GRAIN													
GRAIN													
PASTURE													

MILK PRODUCTION

DOE'S NAME:		IDENTIFICATION:	
BREED:	DATE OF BIRTH:	KIDDING DATE:	

JANUARY		AVERAGE LBS / DAY X 31 DAYS =		LBS
FEBRUARY		AVERAGE LBS / DAY X 31 DAYS =		LBS
MARCH		AVERAGE LBS / DAY X 31 DAYS =		LBS
APRIL		AVERAGE LBS / DAY X 31 DAYS =		LBS
MAY		AVERAGE LBS / DAY X 31 DAYS =		LBS
JUNE		AVERAGE LBS / DAY X 31 DAYS =		LBS
JULY		AVERAGE LBS / DAY X 31 DAYS =		LBS
AUGUST		AVERAGE LBS / DAY X 31 DAYS =		LBS
SEPTEMBER		AVERAGE LBS / DAY X 31 DAYS =		LBS
OCTOBER		AVERAGE LBS / DAY X 31 DAYS =		LBS
NOVEMBER		AVERAGE LBS / DAY X 31 DAYS =		LBS
DECEMBER		AVERAGE LBS / DAY X 31 DAYS =		LBS
YEARLY TOTAL MILK PRODUCED =				LBS

TOTAL VALUE OF MILK PRODUCED FOR THE YEAR

LBS X $		VALUE PER LBS =	

GOAT INFORMATION

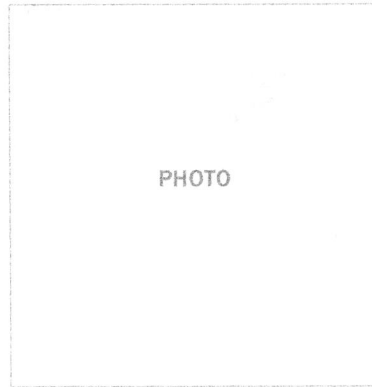

PHOTO

NAME		☐ BUCK	☐ DOE
BREED		BIRTH DATE:	
DATE ACQUIRED:	HOW ACQUIRED: ☐ BORN ON FARM ☐ PURCHASED ☐ LEASED		
COLORS / IDENTIFYING MARKS:			
PURPOSE: ☐ MILK ☐ MEAT ☐ PET ☐ OTHER			

PEDIGREE CHART

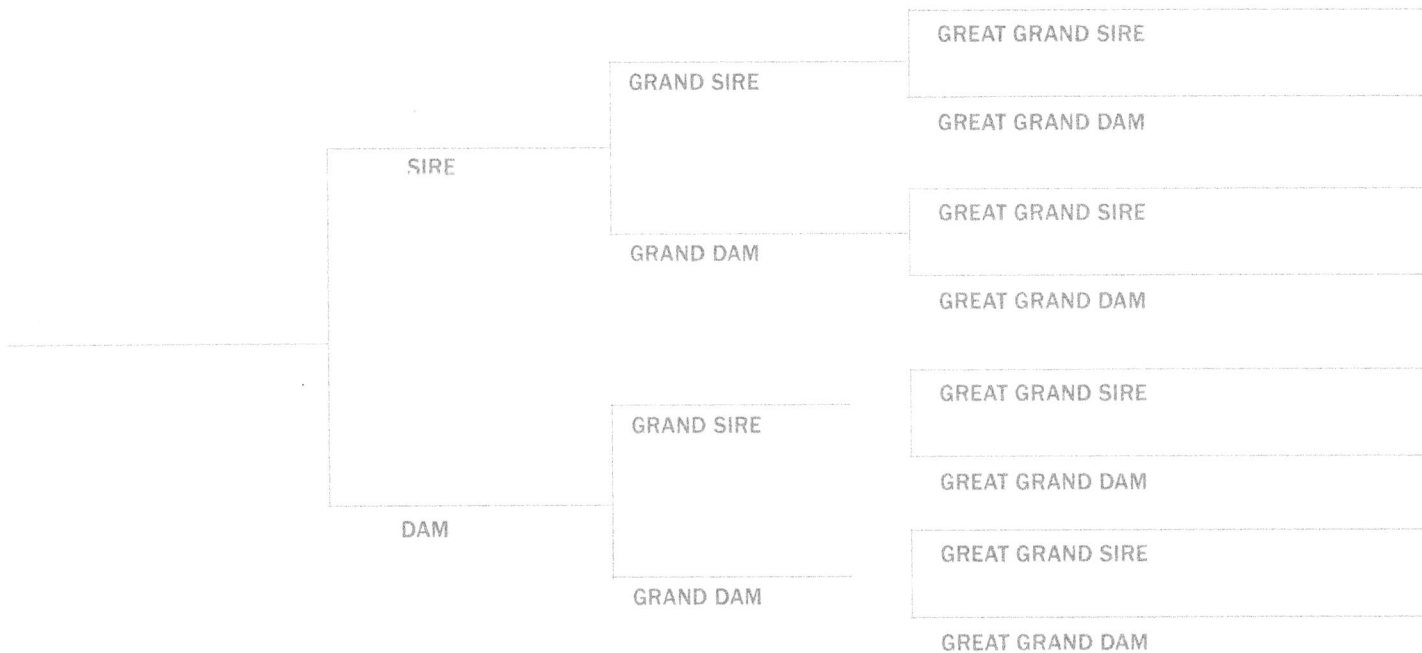

- SIRE
  - GRAND SIRE
    - GREAT GRAND SIRE
    - GREAT GRAND DAM
  - GRAND DAM
    - GREAT GRAND SIRE
    - GREAT GRAND DAM
- DAM
  - GRAND SIRE
    - GREAT GRAND SIRE
    - GREAT GRAND DAM
  - GRAND DAM
    - GREAT GRAND SIRE
    - GREAT GRAND DAM

MEDICAL INFORMATION

INJURY OR ILLNESS

DATE	DESCRIPTION OR NATURE OF ILLNESS	TREATMENT

PARASITE CONTROL

DATE	METHOD OR DEWORMER	DATE	METHOD OR DEWORMER

TESTING RECORD

DATE	TEST PERFORMED (CAE. CL, TB...)	RESULT	DATE	TEST PERFORMED (CAE. CL, TB...)	RESULT

VACCINATION & SUPPLEMENT RECORD

DATE	TARGET DISEASE	DRUG OR SUPPLEMENT USED	DOSAGE	RESULTS

DOE'S KIDDING RECORD

DOE'S NAME:

DATE BREED	KIDDING DATE	# OF KIDS	SEX D/B	NAME OF KID	SIRE OF KID	WEIGHT	TATTOO

BUCK'S RECORD OF PROGENY

DOE'S NAME:

YEAR	BRED TO	KIDS	DOE/BUCK

GOAT RECORD

GOAT'S NAME:

IDENTIFICATION:

BREED:

DATE OF BIRTH:

DATE OF WEANED:

WEIGHT (POUNDS)

BIRTH	JAN	FEB	MAR	APR	MAY	JUN	JUL	AUG	SEP	OCT	NOV	DEC	FINAL

FEED RECORD

	JAN	FEB	MAR	APR	MAY	JUN	JUL	AUG	SEP	OCT	NOV	DEC	TOTAL
GRAIN													
GRAIN													
PASTURE													

MILK PRODUCTION

DOE'S NAME:		IDENTIFICATION:	
BREED:	DATE OF BIRTH:	KIDDING DATE:	

JANUARY		AVERAGE LBS / DAY X 31 DAYS =		LBS
FEBRUARY		AVERAGE LBS / DAY X 31 DAYS =		LBS
MARCH		AVERAGE LBS / DAY X 31 DAYS =		LBS
APRIL		AVERAGE LBS / DAY X 31 DAYS =		LBS
MAY		AVERAGE LBS / DAY X 31 DAYS =		LBS
JUNE		AVERAGE LBS / DAY X 31 DAYS =		LBS
JULY		AVERAGE LBS / DAY X 31 DAYS =		LBS
AUGUST		AVERAGE LBS / DAY X 31 DAYS =		LBS
SEPTEMBER		AVERAGE LBS / DAY X 31 DAYS =		LBS
OCTOBER		AVERAGE LBS / DAY X 31 DAYS =		LBS
NOVEMBER		AVERAGE LBS / DAY X 31 DAYS =		LBS
DECEMBER		AVERAGE LBS / DAY X 31 DAYS =		LBS
YEARLY TOTAL MILK PRODUCED =				LBS

TOTAL VALUE OF MILK PRODUCED FOR THE YEAR

	LBS X $		VALUE PER LBS =	

GOAT INFORMATION

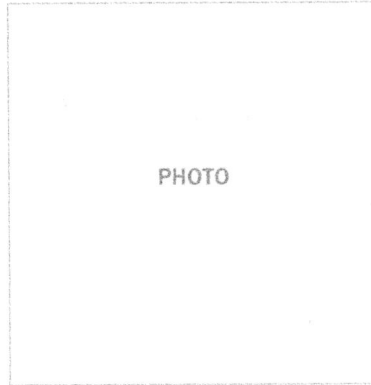

PHOTO

NAME	☐ BUCK	☐ DOE
BREED	BIRTH DATE:	
DATE ACQUIRED:	HOW ACQUIRED: ☐ BORN ON FARM ☐ PURCHASED ☐ LEASED	
COLORS / IDENTIFYING MARKS:		
PURPOSE: ☐ MILK ☐ MEAT ☐ PET ☐ OTHER		

PEDIGREE CHART

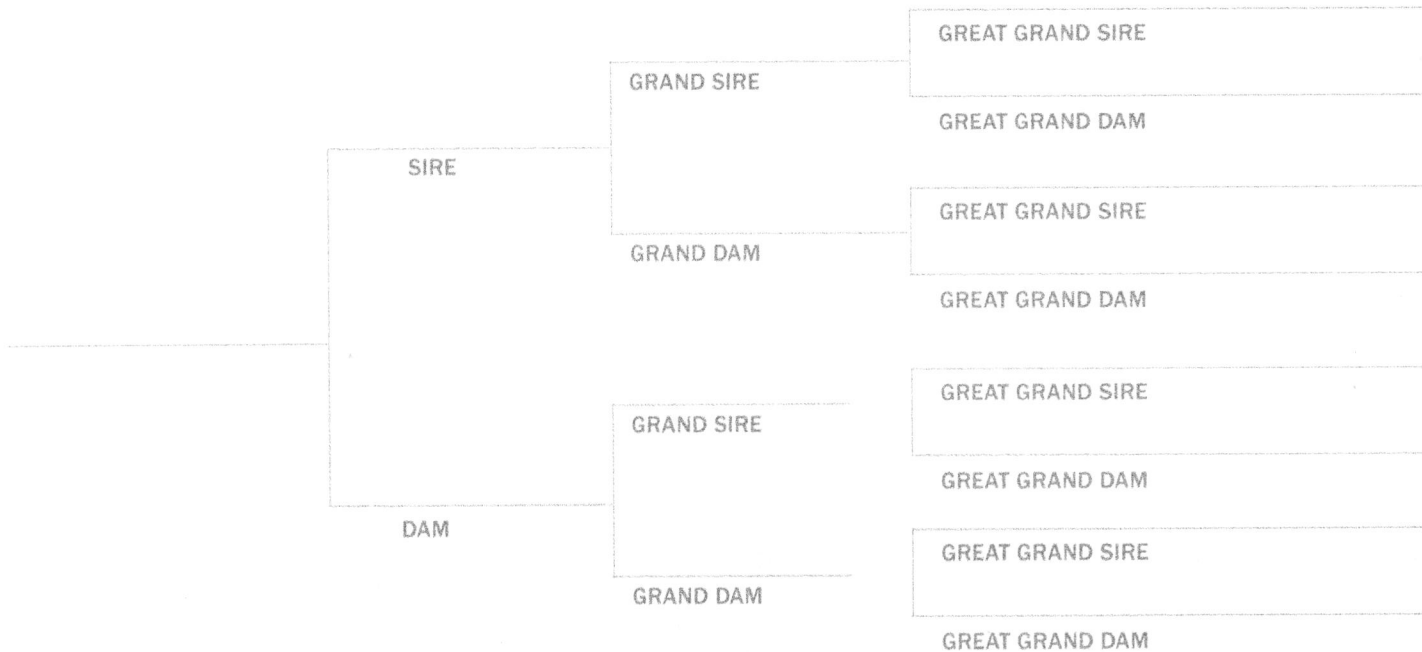

SIRE

GRAND SIRE

GREAT GRAND SIRE

GREAT GRAND DAM

GRAND DAM

GREAT GRAND SIRE

GREAT GRAND DAM

DAM

GRAND SIRE

GREAT GRAND SIRE

GREAT GRAND DAM

GRAND DAM

GREAT GRAND SIRE

GREAT GRAND DAM

MEDICAL INFORMATION

INJURY OR ILLNESS

DATE	DESCRIPTION OR NATURE OF ILLNESS	TREATMENT

PARASITE CONTROL

DATE	METHOD OR DEWORMER	DATE	METHOD OR DEWORMER

TESTING RECORD

DATE	TEST PERFORMED (CAE, CL, TB...)	RESULT	DATE	TEST PERFORMED (CAE, CL, TB...)	RESULT

VACCINATION & SUPPLEMENT RECORD

DATE	TARGET DISEASE	DRUG OR SUPPLEMENT USED	DOSAGE	RESULTS

DOE'S KIDDING RECORD

DOE'S NAME:

DATE BREED	KIDDING DATE	# OF KIDS	SEX D/B	NAME OF KID	SIRE OF KID	WEIGHT	TATTOO

BUCK'S RECORD OF PROGENY

DOE'S NAME:

YEAR	BRED TO	KIDS	DOE/BUCK

GOAT RECORD

GOAT'S NAME:

IDENTIFICATION:

BREED:

DATE OF BIRTH:

DATE OF WEANED:

WEIGHT (POUNDS)

BIRTH	JAN	FEB	MAR	APR	MAY	JUN	JUL	AUG	SEP	OCT	NOV	DEC	FINAL

FEED RECORD

	JAN	FEB	MAR	APR	MAY	JUN	JUL	AUG	SEP	OCT	NOV	DEC	TOTAL
GRAIN													
GRAIN													
PASTURE													

www.ingramcontent.com/pod-product-compliance
Lightning Source LLC
Chambersburg PA
CBHW080559030426
42336CB00019B/3253